How B2B leaders build successful

CUSTOMER-CENTRIC ORGANISATIONS

John O'Connor and Peter Whitelaw

"This is an important book!" - Gavin Patterson, BT Group

First published in 2019

Title: *Customer at the Heart – How B2B leaders build successful Customer-Centric Organisations*

Authors: *John O'Connor and Peter Whitelaw*

ISBN: 978-0-646-99811-4

Published by: Peter Whitelaw Consulting Pty Ltd

A catalogue record for this book is available from the National Library of Australia

Contents

Foreword by Gavin Patterson

This book is important!

A lot of words have been written about putting the 'customer at the heart' but in my experience, it's much harder for business leaders in B2B companies to achieve than you might think, and it certainly takes longer than most people expect.

Early in my career, I spent nine years at Procter & Gamble and that was the starting point for my focus on the 'customer at the heart' because that was fundamental to the way P&G ran its business. In most FMCG companies like Procter, it's intuitive. When I joined the telecommunications industry in the late 1990s, I found very few people who had any real interest in the customer at all. It was all about technology - the product was all important. That's where the power in the value chain was.

Even today, our industry is still playing catch-up. While it's much better than it was 20 years ago, most B2B companies are still not as intuitively customer-centric as they need to be. That's why a book that combines a framework for thinking about customer centricity coupled with the practical experiences of CEOs and business leaders is so useful. A practitioners' guide like this is welcome.

If we as business leaders don't show an interest in customers, nobody else will. It's GE's Jack Welsh who said that if you haven't got a customer, you haven't got a job. That's a very powerful mindset to drive through the organisation so that everybody, both customer-facing and back office, understands that their job is to improve the lives of customers. If they're not looking at their work on a day to day basis through that customer lens, then they're probably not doing the right thing.

I'm a big believer that, as business leaders, we need to start by asking the right questions within our organisations so when our people think about the answers, they start with the customer and end with the customer. As business leaders we also need to supplement our questions with the ability to tell customer stories, to celebrate success, to find the heroes. All these things help set the tone and the tempo for putting the customer at the heart. They give people a sense of priority – a priority for the customer.

Why is priority important? No system is perfect for every situation, so we need our people to be able to fall back on a core set of beliefs. When there isn't a system or procedure to follow, they know that if a customer has an issue, they have the authority to fix it. That where a sense of priority for the customer comes in.

Finally, we need to have patience because putting the customer at the heart takes time – typically years rather than months. The CEO, CFO and Chief People Officer in any company need to keep the faith even when sometimes it feels progress is slow.

Our own journey towards a more customer-centric BT has been a challenging and ultimately rewarding one. I wish you the best in your own journey towards customer centricity.

Gavin Patterson

Chief Executive, BT Group plc (2013-19)

About the Authors

John O'Connor is the CEO of the European B2B customer experience (CX) company Deep-Insight. John has 30 years of experience in customer management. Prior to Deep-Insight, John was an Associate Partner with Accenture in London and led its CX practice in Dublin. John holds an engineering degree from Trinity College Dublin and an MBA from the London Business School. John has advised the senior management of Atos, BT, BUPA, Hitachi, QBE, Toll Group, Renault, Serco, Suncorp and VISA on their CX strategies.

Peter Whitelaw is an Australian consultant providing customer relationship assessments, customer centricity guidance and change management services. Peter has a background in engineering, sales and general management with Hewlett Packard, Tektronix and Optus Communications. For 11 years he was CEO of project and change management training and consulting company Rational Management, training thousands of managers across the world. In recent years he has been lead consultant on several change management and customer centricity projects for both commercial and government organisations.

Acknowledgements

We were fortunate in receiving the co-operation of several leaders in industry and commerce across the world. These interviewees willingly shared their experiences in creating successful customer-centric organisations.

Peter Acheson - Chief Executive Officer, Peoplebank, Melbourne Australia. Now CEO of Chandler Macleod Group, Melbourne.

Peoplebank is Australia's largest provider of IT contract staff and recruitment services operating across Australia and in Singapore and Hong Kong. Peoplebank is a subsidiary of Chandler Macleod Group which is a subsidiary of Recruit Holdings Co. Ltd.

Bob Brown – CIO, Manchester City Council. Also Chair of Info Management and Technology - Manchester Health Locality and holds a Non-Executive Director position as chair of the Industry Advisory Board for Manchester Metropolitan University's business school. Bob is moving to a new role as Chief Solutions Officer at EMIS Health.

Manchester City Council is the local government authority for Manchester, and city and metropolitan borough in Greater Manchester, England (580,000 residents).

Christine Corbett - Group Chief Customer Officer at Australia Post, Melbourne Australia, Now with Pricewaterhouse Coopers.

Australia Post is an Australian government-owned enterprise that provides postal services both locally and internationally, as well as operating retail outlets.

Sue de Wit – Head of Customer Experience, Atos UK & Ireland.

Atos is a leading European IT services corporation with annual revenues of €12 billion and 100,000 employees in 73 countries.

Joe Edwards – Non-Executive Director, Timico. Previously Senior Vice President, Atos.

Timico is a market leading end-to-end Managed Cloud Service Provider. Atos is a leading European IT services corporation with annual revenues of €12 billion and 100,000 employees in 73 countries.

Eamonn Galvin – CEO, Daft.ie., previously held senior executive positions in Accenture, General Electric, eBay and Betfair.

Daft.ie is the number one destination for property searchers and connects property professionals with a unique audience of over 2.5 million users each month. Today, Daft.ie is part of Distilled SCH - the leader in online marketplaces in Ireland.

Lindsay McCaughey – Chief Technology Officer, Galliford Try.

Galliford Try is a British construction company and a FTSE 250 company. It is one of the UK's leading housebuilding, regeneration and construction groups with revenues of £2.8 billion. They operate through three businesses: Linden Homes, Galliford Try Partnerships and Construction & Investments.

Mick McCarthy – CEO, Business and Corporate Banking, Santander Poland.

Santander is one of Europe's largest banks, headquartered in Spain, and is the second largest bank in Poland.

Mairead McSweeney - Head of Business Operations, BT Ireland, Dublin, Ireland.

BT Ireland operates globally and delivers locally, serving multinational corporations, indigenous exporters and public sector organisations in every segment of the Irish economy.

Colm O'Neill – Chief Executive, BT Group plc, London, UK.

BT is one of the world's leading providers of communications services and solutions, serving customers in 180 countries.

Shane O'Neill – Previously Divisional Director, Toll Global Express (an operating division of Toll Group), Sydney, Australia.

Toll Group, now part of Japan Post, is a transportation and logistics company with operations in road, rail, sea, air and warehousing. Toll operates a network of 1,200 sites across 50 countries, with an Asia Pacific focus.

Gavin Patterson – CEO BT, previously with Cable & Wireless (now Virgin Media) and Procter & Gamble.

BT is one of the world's leading providers of communications services and solutions, serving customers in 180 countries.

David Thodey – Chairman, Commonwealth Scientific and Industrial Research Organisation, Sydney, Australia, previously Chief Executive Officer, Telstra Corporation Ltd, Sydney, Australia.

CSIRO is an independent Australian federal government agency responsible for scientific research. Telstra Corporation Ltd. is an Australian telecommunications and media company which builds and operates telecommunications networks and markets voice, mobile, internet access, pay television and other entertainment products and services.

Kathryn Whitehouse – Head of Customer Experience, Major and Public Sector, BT.

BT is one of the world's leading providers of communications services and solutions, serving customers in 180 countries.

Audrey Zibelman – Managing Director and Chief Executive Officer, Australian Energy Market Operator, also Chair, New York Department of Public Service, previously President and CEO of Viridity Energy Inc, Philadelphia USA.

AEMO is responsible for operating Australia's gas and electricity markets and power systems.

Introduction

In order to give you a sense of the ground we are trying to cover in the following pages, it might be helpful to explain why we embarked on a book about customer centricity in business-to-business (B2B) organisations.

The most fundamental element of customer-centricity in the B2B world is being able to deliver a service or solution that meets or exceeds the expectations of the customer in a consistent and repeatable manner. In both of our careers, we have seen companies and their leadership teams struggle with the delivery of what are sometimes viewed as straightforward business services. In theory, these services should be easy to provide but for some reason, they are not.

How difficult can it be for a telecommunications company to deliver data and broadband services in a reliable and consistent fashion? How hard can it be for a transportation company to Deliver a consignment In Full and On Time (DIFOT is a standard measurement metric in the logistics world)? The short answer is: a lot harder than you think. Time and time again, we have seen B2B companies failing to deliver the basic promise of a product or service on time, to specification and within budget.

The challenge of delivering a consistently good service got us thinking about the underlying issues that senior leadership teams face when trying to deliver either a 'basic' business-as-usual offering or, more difficult, to launch a brand-new product line, entering a new market for the first time or onboarding a new client. Most companies and their service providers aspire to building good long-standing working relationships with each other but the inability of service providers to 'do what it says on the tin' consistently is what gives rise to a sense of frustration that can ultimately lead to a breakdown in trust and an undermining of any mutual commitment to make the relationship work. In such cases, the response of many service buyers is to switch suppliers. The response of many service supplier leadership teams and boards is often tactical rather than strategic: replace the CEO or sales director; appoint a Chief Customer Officer; issue an edict that Net Promoter Score (NPS) must be implemented, and so on.

We felt that there had to be a better way to manage B2B customer relationships effectively. To do this would require a framework for analysing the underlying causes of failures in these relationships and for providing a roadmap for leadership teams embarking on a journey to make their organisations more customer-centric.

The subtitle for the book is 'How B2B leaders build successful Customer-Centric Organisations' as we did not want this book to be simply the views of a couple of business consultants, regardless of how many decades of experience we have between us. We wanted to ground this book in the realities that face leadership teams today. To that end, the contents of this book are based on the considered views of CEOs, sales directors and customer experience (CX) leaders in various European and Australian companies. Some of these companies are clients of Deep-Insight, the company that John O'Connor leads; some are business contacts and clients of Peter Whitelaw; others are neither. But all of the people we interviewed have faced the challenges of trying to do the right things for their customers while at same time developing a unique customer-centric DNA for their own organisations.

The title of this book is actually borrowed from a CX programme called 'Client At The Heart' that was established by Ursula Morgenstern when she was CEO for the UK & Ireland division of Atos, a major European IT service provider. Atos is one of the companies we profile in this book. Other companies include AEMO (Australian Energy Market Operator), Australia Post, BT (British Telecom), DAFT, eBay, EMC, HP, Peoplebank, Santander, Toll and Telstra.

In the following pages, we give more prominence to the BT experience for the simple reason that we know the story intimately and we believe it is one of the best examples of how a senior management team with the right leadership and vision can take a company whose heritage is steeped in engineering and product-centricity, and turn it into a truly customer-centric organisation.

The BT story exemplifies the key themes that run through this book:

- Great **Leadership**, and not just from one person but a succession of leaders at various levels within the organisation;
- A clear **Strategy** around the key elements that are important to build a customer-centric company: customers, products and organisation;
- Brilliant **Execution**, from two teams that were led by two 'execution machines' – Mairead McSweeney in BT Ireland and Kathryn Whitehouse in the company's Major and Public Sector division in the UK;
- A customer-centric **Culture** that is still not fully embedded across the organisation yet but the transformation of BT from a product-centric company to a truly customer-centric one is well under way.

We do not claim that BT is the most customer-centric company out there. Far from it. BT's operations in Ireland are now certainly world class in terms of customer centricity but that has been the result of nearly a decade of hard work. BT Major and Public Sector has made great strides in recent years but is still only half-way through its journey to put the customer at the heart of everything it does.

BT is also an example of how a large organisation's journey towards customer centricity can often start in one part of the business before being replicated in other divisions of the same company. In fact, BT provides a lesson for CEOs of large organisations who inevitably find it difficult to create a customer-centric culture in one 'Big Bang.' In most cases, change happens organically and permeates slowly through the organisation but there are mechanisms for speeding up that process, which we will introduce in this book.

The BT story started more than 10 years ago when a new managing director called Chris Clark was appointed to run BT's Irish operations. Clark and subsequent managing directors in Ireland all believed passionately that the journey to financial success must be built around a clear focus on the customer. One of Clark's successors was Colm O'Neill, who accelerated the Customer First programme when he became MD of BT Ireland in 2011. Two years later, Gavin Patterson became Group CEO of BT and while O'Neill was having success in Ireland, Patterson was taking on the challenge of trying to move the entire group from being an engineering-led organisation to being one that was customer-led. By 2015, Patterson was helped by the fact that O'Neill was promoted to run Major and Public Sector (MPS) in the UK, the division that managed BT's relationships with its largest UK private sector and government clients. We follow Colm O'Neill and Gavin Patterson's progress throughout the course of this book.

The framework for creating a customer-centric organisation, which we introduce at the end of Part I, may be our creation but the views and thoughts on how to turn this framework into reality are based primarily on a series of in-depth interviews that we carried out specifically for this book. We are hugely grateful to the individuals from the above organisations who allowed us to interview them for this book: Peter Acheson, Bob Brown, Christine Corbett, Sue de Wit, Joe Edwards, Eamonn Galvin, Mick McCarthy, Lindsay McCaughey, Mairead McSweeney, Colm O'Neill, Shane O'Neill, Gavin Patterson, David Thodey, Kathryn Whitehouse and Audrey Zibelman. Not only did they allow us to interview them, they were incredibly forthright and open in their views and comments. In particular, we need to thank BT's Colm O'Neill for setting up a couple of interviews with clients of BT specifically for this book (see Part VI).

We hope that the result is a practitioner's guide for building customer centricity into the DNA of an organisation. It's also worth saying that much of what we cover in the following pages is not rocket science but neither is any of it straightforward. If it were that easy, all clients would be happy, customer churn would be minimal, and CEOs and sales directors would enjoy much longer tenures than they currently have. The problem is that the delivery of what appears to be a basic service in a B2B organisation is generally far more complex than it appears.

Our hope is that the contents of the following pages will help you on your journey towards a more customer-centric and a more profitable future.

Part I – About Customer Centricity

Chapter 1 – Customer at the Heart

- Definitions
- The Nature of Business Relationships
- Getting the Basics Right
- Customer Relationship Quality (CRQ)
- The Value of Being Customer-Centric
- The Importance of Good Customer Data
- Product-orientation versus Customer-orientation

Chapter 2 – The Role of the Account Manager

- The Central Role of the Account Manager
- The Account Manager as 'Conductor'
- KAMs and GAMs
- Organisational Design

Chapter 3 – Customer Metrics

- Transactional versus Relationship Surveys

Chapter 4 – Net Promoter Score

- The Ultimate Question
- Net Promoter Score – Pros and Cons
- NPS Benchmarking

Chapter 5 – A CX Framework

- Leadership
- Strategy
- Tactics & Execution

- Culture & Change
- A Tale of Two CX Transformation Journeys

Summary of Part I

"We see our customers as invited guests to a party, and we are the hosts. It's our job every day to make every important aspect of the customer experience a little bit better."

- Jeff Bezos, Founder & CEO of Amazon

"A business is simply an idea to make other people's lives better."

- Richard Branson, Founder of Virgin

"In the age of the customer, executives don't decide how customer-centric their companies are — customers do."

- Kate Leggett, Forrester Research

Chapter 1 - Customer at the Heart

Let's start with the challenge that telecommunications companies face – the example we discussed in the Introduction.

Delivering a phone line to a new business premises requires a whole series of activities to be carried out precisely and in sequence: scoping out the work accurately in the first instance, taking the order and processing it on internal IT systems, provisioning the circuits and other equipment, digging up roads to get cables to the client's premises, obtaining permissions from the local authority to dig up that road, and so on. None of these individual tasks is particularly difficult in isolation but stringing these tasks together in a coherent repeatable reliable process is more of a challenge.

If you are a large retailer, you will have multiple outlets that are served by the same telecommunications provider, sometimes in different countries. You will probably be using multiple products from that telecommunications provider as well – broadband as well as data, mobile phones as well as fixed lines, and so on. It gets more complex if the underlying products are supported by different product teams and customer service is provided by different specialists in different geographical locations. Even the process of getting an accurate invoice out to that retailer each month is not that simple when the billing data is held on different billing systems in different countries that invariably do not talk to each other.

This is the day-to-day reality in most B2B organisations. It's not that difficult to be customer-centric if you have a single product delivered to all clients in the same way, using the same technology platform. Very few B2B companies are so lucky. Most are hampered by a myriad of products and product lines, old technologies that require manual intervention, often supported by poorly thought-out processes. Many companies today are the result of mergers that have never been fully integrated. Welcome to the B2B world.

Definitions

Before we launch into the discussion in earnest, it's worth a brief discussion on terminology. Let's start with the term business-to-business (B2B) which refers to a sales or partnership arrangement between two businesses as opposed to business-to-consumer (B2C) which involves selling to individuals.

The main difference between B2B and B2C is that consumer sales – everything from groceries, books, bicycles to perfumes – are focused on meeting the needs of a large number of individual consumers, whereas B2B is based on selling to a smaller number of large accounts. This drives the way marketing, sales and product development are done. Figure 1 below summarises some of the main differences.

Figure 1 – Consumer World versus B2B World

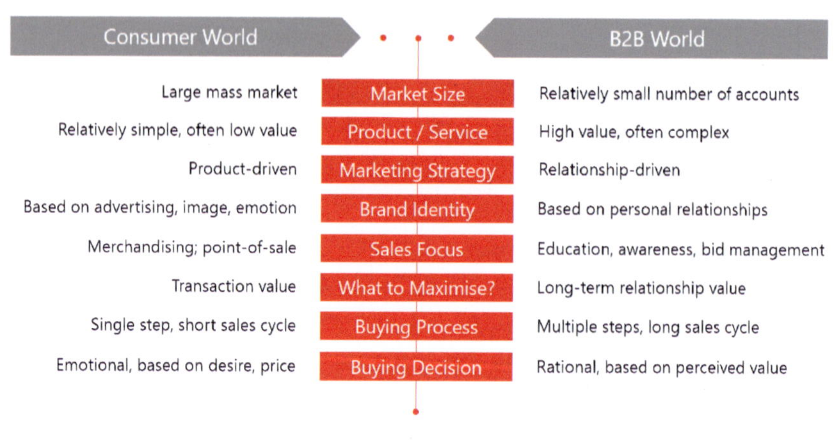

Ultimately the difference between B2B and B2C is relationships and most B2B companies employ people with titles such as relationship manager or account director to manage those business relationships and to increase sales into key accounts.

Like ice creams, B2B also comes in several different flavours. B2G refers to selling to, or partnering with, government and public sector organisations. Most of the principles remain the same but there are subtle differences in how procurement and tendering is carried out. B2B2C (business to business to consumer) refers to selling through distributors, wholesalers or channel partners. For example, selling your insurance products through brokers or selling food and clothing items through retailers is a B2B2C activity. Who is the real customer? The answer is clearly both: the insurance company must create a product that end-customers will want but the insurer must also get inside the minds of its brokers in order to figure out how to persuade them to push its product rather than those of its competitors. Increasing the share of wallet is the name of the game here but in most respects, the same rules apply.

In this book, we talk about customer experience (CX) programmes and capturing the Voice of the Customer (VOC). But is Customer eXperience Management (CXM) the same as Customer Relationship Management (CRM) and frankly does it even matter? A 2018 study by CustomerThink looked at some of these questions and found considerable overlap amongst practitioners. They were asked if they agree or disagree with the following statements:

Statement	Agree
CXM can't succeed without engaged employees	100%
CXM is a business strategy for creating loyal customer relationships	97%
CXM means delivering the brand promise	90%
CXM includes any effort to improve customer satisfaction	89%
By 2020, customer experience will overtake price and product as the key brand differentiator	74%
CX initiatives must include products and pricing	65%
CXM requires and a Chief Customer/Experience Officer to be successful	52%
The primary goal of CXM is to improve customer service	31%
To be successful, CXM should just focus on making experiences easy	24%
CXM is another term for a Voice of the Customer programme	23%
CXM is difficult because customer perceptions can't be "managed"	15%
CXM is the same as Customer Success Management	13%
CXM is a replacement for Customer Relationship Management	13%

Bob Thompson of CustomerThink says that "the implication for CX leaders is that key stakeholders may — and probably do — have widely varying perceptions about CX and CXM. Some may think of CXM in a holistic way, but others may believe that CX is just another term for customer service, process improvement, or customer surveys".

We are very much in the holistic camp and this was borne out by the interviews with various CEOs and sales directors that we interviewed for this book. As a general rule, they viewed CX or CXM as a fundamental transformation of their organisations to make them truly customer-facing. Essentially, they were talking about major change programmes that involved every function in their companies, not just the customer-facing ones. David Thodey from Telstra explained to us why customer experience is so much more than just customer service. Customer surveys are only one tiny part of that transformation story that our interviewees talked about.

The Nature of Business Relationships

In the B2B world, business relationships are based more on a partnership between two organisations rather than a pure buyer-supplier approach. Sure, there are cases where the buyer is purchasing a commodity product and is not really interested in developing a long-term relationship but in our experience these cases are few and far between. Even where the underlying product or service is a commodity, there are other factors at play. For example, GasTerra is a Dutch company involved in the wholesale of natural gas to energy companies and large industrial organisations. It is 50 percent owned by the Dutch government, 25 percent by Shell and 25 percent ExxonMobil. It is the sole buyer of gas from the Groningen gas fields in the Netherlands.

On the face of it, GasTerra is a commodity organisation. Scratch beneath the surface and it becomes clear that GasTerra's customers are interested in more than just the lowest price. Security of supply is of critical importance to many industrial clients, so a long-term contract is more than just a commercial agreement based on price alone. Other clients have requirements to have energy delivered from green sources such as biogas or other sources of non-fossil origin. Others require flexible solutions regarding contractual obligations, options and invoicing. It might seem strange but many of GasTerra's customers have specifically stated that they are looking for a partnership approach rather than commodity supplier arrangement.

So, what does a good partnership arrangement like? In our view, the three fundamental pillars of any good business relationship are:

- **Commitment**. As we have seen from the GasTerra example, commitment to a long-term two-way partnership is a key objective for most B2B relationships. Commitment is the cornerstone of any loyal partnership.
- **Trust**. Long-term relationships are built upon a basis of fairness and honesty between both parties. This requires give and take on both sides and a willingness to go beyond the confines of any underpinning commercial agreement if the situation demands it.
- **Satisfaction**. Satisfaction is the outcome of meeting or exceeding a client's expectations for the delivery of a certain product, service or solution. Although it is more 'transactional' than Commitment or Trust, it is nonetheless a key element of any business relationship.

We have already mentioned that most B2B companies have good relationships with the majority of their clients. Figure 2 shows what a typical client portfolio should look like. These figures are based on nearly 20 years of data from Deep-Insight – all from B2B companies – across Europe and Australia (together with some North American organisations).

Figure 2 – Typical B2B Customer Portfolio (segmented by Relationship Type)

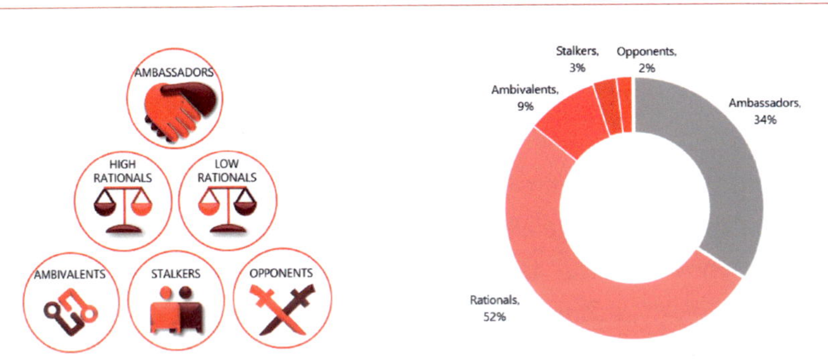

In a typical client portfolio, one third of accounts are *Ambassadors* that think the service they receive is unique. Ambassadors are great advocates for your company and are generally prepared to pay a premium because, in their view, there is nobody else in the market who can deliver as good a product or service in as consistent or reliable a fashion. It is difficult or impossible for competitors to muscle in on the territory.

The largest number of clients in any client portfolio are typically *Rational* in nature. They don't see you or your offering as unique but they are generally happy with the product or service offering and, all other things considered, will stay in the business relationship for the foreseeable future. They may look around at alternative sources of supply from time to time but unless something dramatic happens to switch the balance of power (change of CEO, takeover by another company, etc.) the relationship should continue.

At the bottom end of the *Rational* category are clients that are starting to display *Ambivalent* views on the client relationship. They are ambivalent in that they love the business solution on offer but hate the experience or, more commonly, they like the people they deal with but the product or service on offer fails to meet the needs of their business. If the solution or the experience is poor, the business relationship becomes more fragile and clients start to think about moving.

As we move into *Stalker* or *Opponent* territory, the relationship has broken down and sometimes the situation is irretrievable. Very often, the root cause is poor delivery of the underlying product or service. If the root cause of the breakdown is identified and the problem addressed quickly, a *Stalker* or *Opponent* may become a *Rational* again. We see this happen frequently when a senior leadership team makes a conscious decision to win back a large client that is on the point of defection. This often involves the implementation of a Service Improvement Plan (SIP) but will usually also include members of the senior leadership team 'love-bombing' the client in an effort to rebuild the relationship.

Getting the Basics Right

Most employees want to do a good job for their customers. Most organisations pride themselves on giving great service to their clients. So why is it so hard to create a truly customer-centric culture in organisations today? And it is a genuine challenge for many B2B firms. We know this to be the case from the customer feedback that we gather on behalf of B2B companies over a period of two decades. Customers rarely complain about price, but they do comment about poor value-for-money. They also complain about product and service providers not being proactive, being overly bureaucratic, and just not being customer-focused. Interestingly, the most common issue that we see – and this comes from analysing customer feedback for nearly two decades, is the failure to meet client expectations and deliver the basic promise of an on time, within budget.

Typical customer verbatim quotes:

"Greatest Weakness? Their failure to deliver."

"Processes not as efficient as they could be i.e. length of time it takes for a Work Request Proposal to be issued to the client"

"The lead time for delivery of new and changes to existing services is very slow. The service desk that supports us with our issues at times feels like it provides no value. Updates to issues are slow and inconclusive"

"Not living up to promises in bid in terms of level of support and responsiveness to customer needs" "Project management leaves a lot to be desired. We've had a plethora of PMs, all of whom repeat the same phrase over and over, as if it somehow mitigates any responsibility: 'Sorry, I'm not technical.' Projects that should take 3 months take in excess of a year part due to things like this, but also lack of resources and not having a PM capable of identifying what resource is required."

"End to end business processes need some improvement to ensure they are synchronised across the account."

"Billing is atrocious; incorrect details on invoices, details missing from invoices, discounts missing from invoices. Delivery of services is poor as well. Prolonged delivery times, poor communications relating to installation of services."

All of the above quotes are actual verbatim comments from real people at the receiving end of bad products or poor service. Even from a quick glance at these verbatims, it's clear that the issues are varied and there is unlikely to be a silver bullet that will solve all issues within any individual account. Multiply that by hundreds or thousands of accounts and the challenge for any leadership team becomes exponentially harder.

Customer Relationship Quality (CRQ)

One way of looking at business relationships is via the following model.

Figure 3 – Key Elements of a Good B2B Partnership

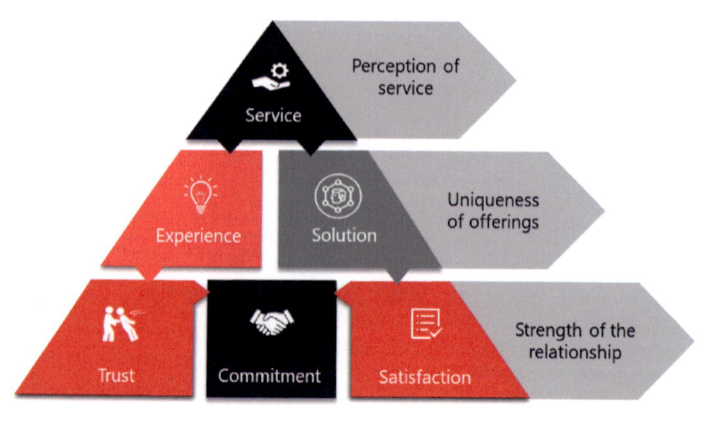

As we have mentioned earlier, the key elements of any business relationship are Trust, Commitment and Satisfaction but these are only the outcomes of how good the product or solution is perceived by the client, and how good the client feels about the experience of working with that service provider. When we talk about 'Solution' we are really talking about concepts like being seen as leading edge in the marketplace, being innovative and providing good value for money.

'Experience' encompasses concepts like ease of doing business and being a true business partner. The uniqueness of the solution and the experience are dependent on the underpinning service that is provided. It's hard to be seen as unique if you are delivering an inconsistent or a poor service so it is really important to get the basics right.

At this point, we should declare a personal interest in this model. Deep-Insight was founded in 2000 with the specific objective of measuring the quality of relationships between two B2B partners using the *Customer Relationship Quality (CRQ)* methodology. We are not trying to push our CRQ approach in this book – at least not blatantly. In fact, we will spend much more time discussing a metric called Net Promoter Score (NPS) as it has become the de facto standard in measuring customer loyalty today.

The Value of Being Customer-Centric

At this point, one might be tempted to ask "why worry about all these challenges and difficulties?" After all, if every company suffers from similar problems, then surely it all evens out in the end? You lose a few clients here because they are dissatisfied with your service. You pick up some other clients over there because they are equally dissatisfied with their current product or service provider. It's swings and roundabouts. What's the big deal? Isn't that's just how business works?

For many senior leadership teams, the reason is often a personal and selfish one. Shareholders and company boards are more demanding in the 21st century than they were in the 20th. Even if the majority of client issues are related to service delivery, the two people who are often most in the firing line are the CEO and the sales director. These two individuals are ultimately responsible for achieving the profit and revenue targets set for them by the board. The tenure of senior executives is shorter now than it ever was. If a sales director isn't meeting his or her targets, the axe drops more quickly than it has ever done in the past. One source reckons that the average tenure of a sales director in now 19 months compared to 26 months in 2010.

There is also a very compelling commercial reason. More than 20 years ago, a partner from the American strategy consultancy Bain & Co wrote a book called *The Loyalty Effect*. It became an instant bestseller, primarily because the author Fred Reichheld declared some obvious truths about sales and customer value. He proposed that it is a whole lot easier to sell to an existing customer than to find a new one. Seven times easier, according to Reichheld. He also found that loyal customers are also less expensive to serve than non-loyal customers. Loyal customers are more likely to pay a premium for products and services than a non-loyal customer. They are also more willing to provide positive word-of-mouth references – in effect, they become part of your company's marketing machine.

One of the statistics that Reichheld promoted in his book was a claim that a five percent increase in customer retention rates can increase the value of that customer by anywhere from 25 percent to 100 percent, depending on the industry you operate in. Reichheld's fundamental premise was that companies needed to think about the lifetime value of customers rather than the value of an individual transaction. Reichheld was saying nothing new here – academics in Europe like Gronroos and Gummesson had been saying the same thing for years. The difference is that Reichheld and Bain had greater influence at boardroom level than the academic community.

In 2003, Bain and Fred Reichheld took the argument one step further and created a customer metric called the Net Promoter Score (NPS) but more on that topic shortly.

The Importance of Good Customer Data

Thirty years ago, when one of the authors was starting out on a consulting career in the UK and the other was a sales manager for a technology company in Australia, the business world was a different place. The Internet hadn't been invented; there were no mobile phones; laptops were not yet commonplace; business meetings were recorded on Dictaphones and typed up by secretaries. That said, business decisions were not just based on gut feel. Facts and figures were important. Customer research was conducted – by telephone rather than by email or via the Web – and the results analysed in a similar fashion to today. The analysis tools were the precursors of today's ubiquitous Microsoft Excel spreadsheet: VisiCalc and Lotus 1-2-3. However, it was the introduction of the IBM PC Convertible in 1986 and Microsoft's launch of an IBM-compatible version of Excel the following year that started to put analysis tools into the hands of the business community and shifted the power base away from the central IT department which still controlled the company mainframe and most of the key financial and customer data.

A new role was created in many organisations – that of the 'business analyst'. In the 1990s, these business analysts were employed by all major organisations, helping senior business executives make decisions based on ad-hoc analyses of financial, product and customer data. It was a great time to be alive if you were a business analyst, because without these ad-hoc analytical projects, nobody at a senior level in the organisation had the remotest idea of how profitable a particular customer or account was, or even if a particular customer segment was profitable or loss-making.

One of the authors (John) remembers working as a consultant on a strategic project for a UK bank and after three months of analysis, the consulting team presented its conclusions to the bank's executive team: the bank should concentrate on its business banking customers and shut down its retail banking operations. The reason was simple: even if the bank could reduce the cost of servicing its entire retail customers by 50 percent, the retail division would still be unprofitable. The executive team was astounded. They had no idea that the retail banking division was terminally loss-making. The executive team took the news on the chin and started the preparations for shedding the majority of their customers, in order to concentrate on providing a more focused service to the 10 percent who actually generated a profit for the bank. It was a salutary reminder of the importance of fact-based decision-making in business, as well as the criticality of good customer segmentation and good customer data.

Product-orientation versus Customer-orientation

One other memory from that UK banking project was the realisation that most companies were organised along product lines rather than by customer segment. The reason was due to technology and IT limitations as much as anything else. Most banks had built one software application to manage deposits and a completely different application to manage loans. Mortgages were just a different type of loan but the term of the loan was 25 or 30 years, these mortgages were often managed on a completely different IT system. Similarly, in the manufacturing world, different production lines would be set up for the production of different products. A customer might purchase three products from the manufacturing company but they would be registered as three separate customers on the manufacturer's computer systems.

It seems crazy now but not that long ago, very few organisations had a single view of the customer. At the time, it was difficult to work out product profitability but it was almost impossible to calculate customer profitability, simply because nobody knew with any degree of accuracy how many customers a company had. By way of example, one of the leading banks in Ireland had more than six million customers on its books at the time, despite the fact that there were fewer than five million people on the island of Ireland. Customers were double-counted or triple-counted if they had more than one banking product with the bank. In the absence of reliable data on how many customers a company had, customer segmentation in the 1980s and 1990s was more of a guessing game than a science.

Today, customer segmentation is more scientific, and the analysis tools and techniques used to make business decisions can be extremely sophisticated. So why the history lesson? In short, while today's analysis tools might be sophisticated, many traditional businesses still operate along 1980s organisational lines. Put simply, many B2B companies still have a product rather than customer mentality and this product-based approach determines how activities are carried out within the organisation. BT's CEO Gavin Patterson thinks this is changing rapidly but is still a challenge for companies today.

Gavin Patterson: It has changed in the 15 years, and it's even changed in my five years as CEO making sure that systems and processes are designed with the customer in mind first and foremost. One of the challenges in all telecom companies – and in banks the same – is that the systems were designed around products originally and not around customers.

This product-based approach has many unintended consequences. It still surprises us to see successful modern-day companies sending three separate account managers to visit the same client, simply because that client deals with three different divisions within the company and each division has its own sales and account team. Despite the technological advances in the past three decades, few B2B companies have truly created a Single Point of Contact (SPOC) for every client. In such cases, the account managers are not managing the account. They become glorified order takers for individual products that are sold into that account.

This brings us neatly to the role of the account manager in making a company truly customer centric.

Chapter 2 – The Role of the Account Manager

Account managers are called different things in different companies. And in different countries. Sometimes they are referred to as sales managers although less so in Europe than in America. In Europe, 'selling' is still regarded as a second-class profession and the 'salesman' is a person who deals in used cars or snake oil.

Across the pond in North America, sales is a true profession and most of the today's sales techniques and approaches have been developed in the USA. In the 1970s, an IBM national account salesman named Stephen Heiman joined up with Robert Miller to form the Miller-Heiman Group which popularised the concepts of *strategic selling* and *conceptual selling*. They believed that sales people needed to understand the client's buying process and manage the various decision makers in that process, rather than simply making a sales pitch. *SPIN selling* was another American sales approach invented by Neil Rackham in the 1980s. Rackham broke the sales process into four stages: Situation, Problem, Implication and Need-Payoff. There are many other sales approaches and methodologies.

In Europe, the term account manager (or some variation thereof) is more frequently used than salesperson. In Australia, business development manager (BDM) is a commonly used term. The titles may be different, but the roles are generally similar and involve client management as well as increasing the level of sales within a particular account or portfolio of clients. For very large clients, there may be a single account manager dedicated to the account. In most cases, the account manager will have a portfolio that might range from 5 to 50 accounts. The decision as to whether an account manager should have a portfolio of one, five or 50 accounts is an important strategic one.

To illustrate this point, consider Joe Edwards, the sales director for Atos UK & Ireland whom we interviewed for this book. Edwards started his sales career with Hewlett-Packard (HP) where one of his clients was Boots, the pharmaceutical and retailing company. After about a year in the role, the senior management at HP made the strategic decision to reclassify Boots as a key account as they believed it had significant sales potential.

Joe Edwards: After about a year as a sales executive at HP and having a dozen or so accounts, the company turned around and said, 'Actually, Joe, we just want you to focus on Boots Pharmaceuticals, and we're going to double your quota.'

I learned that I was skimming the surface with Boots for a year and it was nice and comfortable because I had lots of other accounts I could fall back on if I wasn't getting the numbers out of Boots. Then the company then said: you don't have a choice; you either make your numbers out of Boots, or you don't. That drives a very different set of behaviours, and I thought to myself: "how am I going to do this?"

We pick up Joe Edwards' story in the Part III of this book (Strategy) as one of the most fundamental strategic decisions a company can make in its journey towards customer-centricity is the segmentation of its clients. Not all clients should be treated equally. Some deserved a dedicated account manager; others are ideally served by a telephone- or desk-based team, simply because of the economics of managing different categories of clients. That doesn't mean smaller clients are treated badly; it just means they are treated appropriately.

The Central Role of the Account Manager

Perhaps more than anybody else in a B2B company, the account manager has the most pivotal role in the client relationship. If you are a CEO, Chief Customer Officer or Customer Experience (CX) Director attempting to create a truly customer-centric culture in your company, the account manager is your key to success. Win over the account teams and customer-centricity is easy to achieve. Fail to get the account teams on side and the entire CX programme is doomed to failure. It's as simple as that.

The central role of the account manager may be self-evident but it's worth recalling some of the evidence for this. From our own research we know that the views of customers on any company are very strongly correlated with the customers' views on the account manager.

Figure 4 – Correlation between Account Management Index and Customer Relationship Quality

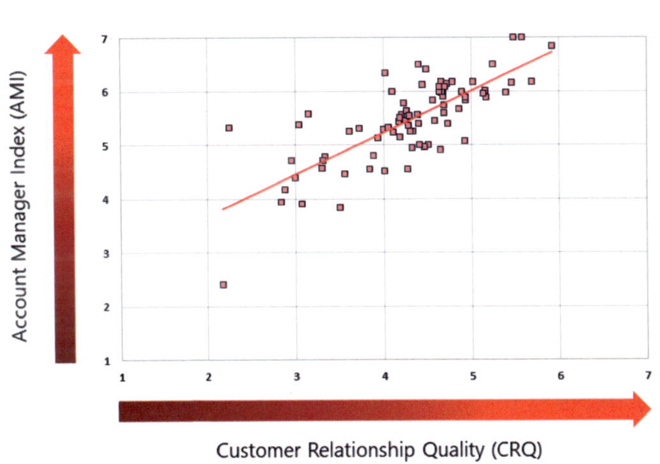

Figure 4 shows this correlation for a large UK company with more than 1,000 clients managed by nearly 80 account managers. Each dot on the chart represents an account manager. The Account Manager Index (AMI) score for that account manager is the aggregate view of what that account manager's clients think of her (essentially, is she good, trustworthy and reliable). The Customer Relationship Quality (CRQ) score for that account manager is the aggregate view of how the account manager's clients view the relationship with the service provider. In general, the client's views on the service provider tend to be positive if the client has a 'good' account manager but some interpretation is required with such scores. A poor CRQ score does not always mean a poor account manager. Sometimes, the best account managers are assigned the larger or more problematic client relationships.

This gets to the heart of the relationship between the client and account manager. Even though the account manager cannot be held responsible for the quality of the product being supplied or the service delivered to the client, that client's views on both the service provider and the account manager are remarkably consistent. Good account managers make for better, longer-lasting client relationships.

The Account Manager as 'Conductor'

We like to use the analogy of an orchestra to describe good account management. The conductor doesn't play the instruments, but he does assemble the best musicians and encourage them – by whatever means – to deliver the best result for the audience. The Austrian Herbert von Karajan is often regarded as one of the best conductors of the 20th century. Fellow conductor Mariss Jansons described him as follows: *"Often in rehearsal Karajan didn't conduct. The art was to make the orchestra listen to itself. Critics sniped but, for musicians, what he did bordered on the miraculous."* Von Karajan has also been described as authoritative, steely and even ruthless. A good account manager needs some of these traits as well but also needs to have empathy with people in order to get the best out of them.

The British conductor Simon Rattle is seen as one the current greats and for the purposes of this analogy, maybe a better example of a perfect conductor. A man of great energy and huge enthusiasm, Rattle also understood the power and importance of audience feedback. In an interview in 2010, he said: *"If you receive a whole string of bad reviews, you have to say, 'OK, maybe there's something here we should pay attention to.'"* Good account managers are not afraid of client feedback. They embrace it, as ultimately it becomes the mechanism by which they understand the needs of their clients and sell them more. We return to this theme in Parts IV and V of this book ('Tactics & Execution' and 'Culture & Change') when we discuss the importance of getting the complete and enthusiastic buy-in from the sales and service communities.

KAMs and GAMs

Account managers, like ice creams, come in different flavours, shapes and sizes. Invariably they also come with TLAs, or three-letter acronyms, including key account manager (KAM) and global account manager (GAM). It's a confusing area as there are few clear-cut definitions as to what key account management actually means. In her book Key Account Management, Diana Woodburn describes it as *"a supplier-led process of inter-organisational collaboration that creates unique value for both supplier and strategically important customers".* The inter-organisational collaboration reference brings us back to the conductor analogy – the KAM needs to be able to bring the best elements from across the organisation to bear on the account. This is not an easy thing to achieve if the company is organised around product lines. The challenge is far greater for GAMs if they have to navigate their way across both product and geographical borders. Here we get to another of those organisational challenges of becoming customer-centric. If your client is international or global and wants to work on an international or global basis with its suppliers, it is simply not possible to be truly customer-centric if your company is organised along country lines and where a global account management function cannot be put in place. Again, it may seem a trivial exercise to establish GAM capability. It is not trivial if your financial systems report revenues and profits by country rather than by client. Neither is it trivial if the global account manager is based in Sydney, reporting to an Australian managing director, but most of the client contacts and decision-making is in London.

We address this point again in the 'Strategy' section of this book.

Organisational Design

Peter Whitelaw likes to ask the following question in his workshops with senior executives:

"What do you consider to be your greatest asset?"

Most executives immediately say "our staff" and they may well be right. Without good high-performing staff, it's pretty difficult to design, manufacture and sell products or services that exceed the expectations of customers on a consistent basis. In some of Peter's workshops, the executives will say "the customer" but in truth, these cases are the exception rather than the rule.

It's the customer that pays the wages of the staff who are designing, manufacturing and selling the company's products but in many organisations those staff are rarely if ever engaged in working with the customer in the design and development of the next range of products. Sometimes the voices of the customers are heard when they complain loudly enough about the existing product or service but few companies truly integrate the customer's perspective into the inner workings of the organisation. The customer is rarely represented at the meetings where products, processes and services and reviewed.

Amazon's Jeff Bezos famously asks for an empty chair to be left at the table at all senior management meetings to remind the attendees that there is another person in the room whose views must be represented at that meeting – the customer. It may sound cheesy but it's a simple and effective way to remind people that the customer is king. Throughout this book, we provide examples of how B2B business leaders try to ensure that the customer's voice is always heard above the day-to-day noise that is present in every organisation. In Part II (Leadership) we will see how CEOs like BT's Gavin Patterson and Telstra's David Thodey have tried to instil customer centricity into their organisations. We will see how Atos' Ursula Morgenstern takes personal ownership of the customer agenda. But exhortation and personal ownership by CEOs is not enough. More systematic approaches are also needed. In Part III (Strategy) we examine how companies like Australia Post have created a new position called the Chief Customer Officer to allow the voice of the customer to be heard at the highest level in the organisation. In Part III, we also look at how organisational design is necessary to ensure that a company's key customers or global customers are assigned the appropriate level of account management, and how key account management (KAM) and global account management (GAM) require structural changes to be made within the company if KAM and GAM are to work.

In Part IV (Tactics & Execution), we look at how these organisational designs can be implemented in practice, and in Part V (Culture & Change) we will explore how to use organisational design to embed a customer-centric philosophy and culture into the DNA of the organisation.

Chapter 3 - Customer Metrics

"What gets measured, gets managed" is a famous phrase attributed to management guru Peter Drucker. His 1954 book *The Practice of Management* is a classic management text, but the phrase does not appear anywhere in the book which in itself is a lesson about checking the accuracy and sources of data – particularly customer data. Drucker does have a lot to say about the gathering and use of customer feedback to inform management decisions. His words are as valid today as when he wrote it in 1954:

> Peter Drucker: Service performance should never be appraised by management guesses or on the basis of occasional chats the 'big boss' has with important customers. It should be measured by regular, systematic and unbiased questioning of the customer. In a large company this may have to take the form of an annual customer survey. The outstanding job here has probably been done by General Motors; and it explains the company's success in no small degree. In the small company the same results can be achieved by a different method.

The key phrase here is "regular, systematic and unbiased questioning of the customer" and it's worth examining its elements carefully:

- **Regular**. Many companies get customer feedback on an ad-hoc basis. There's nothing wrong with ad hoc feedback but if you want your people and your clients to get into a rhythm or a cadence of providing and acting on customer feedback, it has to be done on a regular basis. We'll discuss this in more detail in the 'Strategy' and 'Tactics & Execution' parts of this book.

- **Systematic**. This is linked to the above. If you want to understand if things are trending in the right direction, the approach to questioning the customer must be exactly the same this time as last time – same process; same approach; same questions. More about this in 'Tactics & Execution'.
- **Unbiased**. Ideally, a third party should be involved rather than the account manager. Again, we will cover the options and the pros and cons of each in "Tactics & Execution".
- **Questioning of the customer**. What questions? Open-ended or closed? By whom?

Drucker also talks about the importance of face-to-face discussions at the most strategic level with customers.

> Peter Drucker: In one of the most successful hospital-supply wholesalers, two of the top men of the company – president and chairman of the Board – visit between them two hundred of the company's six hundred customers every year. They spend a whole day with each customer. They do not sell – refuse indeed to take an order. They discuss the customer's problems and his needs and ask for criticism of the company's products and service. In this company the annual customer survey is considered the first job of top management. And the company's eighteen-fold growth in the last twelve years is directly attributed to it.

Note that phrase *"In this company the annual customer survey is considered the first job of top management."* We'll come back to this phrase in Part II when we discuss the importance of Leadership in creating a customer-centric organisation.

Transactional versus Relationship Surveys

At this point, it's worth making a clear distinction between three different types of customer survey. The annual customer survey that Drucker talks about is a strategic assessment of the overall relationship and is designed first and foremost to facilitate a deeper understand of the company's business and its needs so that any products or services sold to that company are fit for purpose and will meet or exceed expectations.

This is very different to the regular transactional surveys that we all experience from time to time – the text message that is sent to customers from Vodafone every time their support desk is contacted which is used to evaluate the quality of the service provided on that particular transaction. Or the monthly questionnaire that IT staff get from an external IT service provider to evaluate if the service level agreement (SLA) is being achieved. These questions and surveys are very transactional in nature and serve the (very valuable) purpose of monitoring the ongoing provision of a service so that any operational issues are identified immediately and resolved quickly.

In some instances, a hybrid model is required. For example, a construction fit-out company may have an ongoing relationship with a major retailer to upgrade its entire portfolio of stores. Each store upgrade is a project in its own right, which might last six weeks or six months but deserves to be tracked separately. The Operations Director needs to know how each project is progressing and can't afford to wait for the annual relationship assessment to understand if Project A or Project B is in trouble.

The three types of survey are depicted in Figure 5.

Most good CX programmes will use a combination of survey type but it is important to understand that the annual strategic relationship survey is critical to understanding how the partnership should be developed. When used correctly, that relationship survey becomes a highly effective account management tool rather than an exercise in market research.

Figure 5 – Relationship verses Episodic versus Transactional Surveys

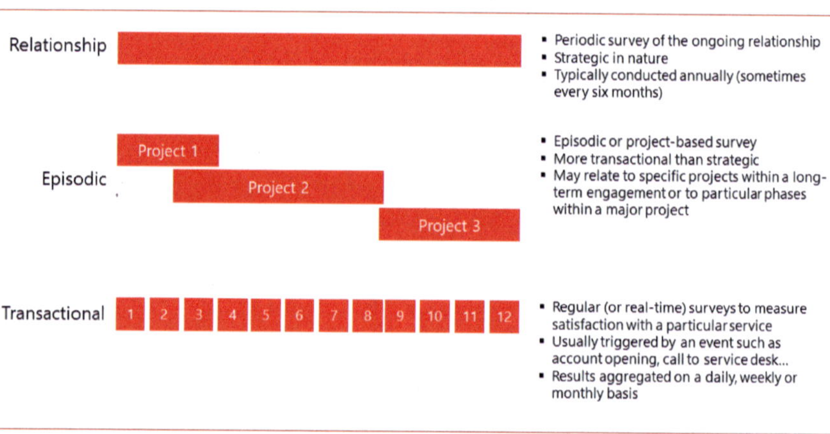

Chapter 4 – Net Promoter Score

In *The Practice of Management* Drucker has little or nothing to say about customer metrics or what questions should be asked of customers as part of the survey process. In 1954, the practice of customer research was not well developed. Strange as it may seem, it was only in the 1970s that customer satisfaction research emerged as a legitimate field of enquiry. Since then, a plethora of approaches and methodologies have been created to measure customer satisfaction and loyalty.

The Ultimate Question

As we mentioned earlier, Fred Reichheld created the Net Promoter Score (NPS) metric in 2003 which was essentially an advocacy measure based on a single question: *"Would you recommend Company X to a friend or colleague?"* Reichheld followed this up with a book called *The Ultimate Question* which argued that NPS was the only question you needed to ask of customers in order to figure out if they were going to be loyal or not. Across the world, boards were beginning to focus more intently on customer loyalty, and many were pushing the executive teams to adopt NPS as a metric that could measure loyalty and help drive profitable growth.

Fred Reichheld: Whenever a customer feels misled, mistreated, ignored, or coerced, then profits from that customer are bad. Bad profits come from unfair or misleading pricing. Bad profits arise when companies save money by delivering a lousy customer experience. Bad profits are about extracting value from customers, not creating value. When sales reps push overpriced or inappropriate products onto trusting customers, the reps are generating bad profits. When complex pricing schemes dupe customers into paying more than necessary to meet their needs, those pricing schemes are contributing to bad profits.

Within a few years, NPS had gained a lot of traction in corporate boardrooms in America as a valid customer loyalty metric. It also attracted some heavy criticism – in particular from one researcher called Tim Keiningham who gave NPS a particularly scathing review saying that he and his research team could find no evidence for the claims made by Reichheld. It should be said that Keiningham worked for the market research company Ipsos so his views may not be completely unbiased.

At that time, our own view in Deep-Insight was that NPS was probably too simplistic a metric for B2B companies, and that Deep-Insight's own CRQ methodology, which also included an advocacy question, was a better fit for complex business relationships. If we are being completely honest, there was an element of 'Not Invented Here' at play so at the time we decided to ignore NPS as a useful B2B metric.

But here's the thing: our customers didn't agree with us. When we ran customer feedback programmes for customers like Reed Elsevier and Atos in the UK, ABN AMRO in the Netherlands, Santander in Poland, and the Toll Group in Australia, they all said to us: *"Can you add in the NPS question for us – we have to report the numbers back to headquarters?"* and we always obliged.

Ten years later, NPS still hadn't gone away. If anything, it had become even more popular, particularly with large international companies where a simple understandable metric was needed to compare results across different divisions and geographical areas. And when we finally looked into it, we discovered that Deep-Insight had actually been gathering NPS data from our clients' customers across 86 different countries. Around the same time, we also did some research into our own database to find out what really drove loyalty and profitability in our clients. Now this is not an easy thing to do, as many of you who have tried will know, but where we had several years of customer feedback data, it was relatively straightforward to analyse how many of our clients' B2B customers were still with them, and for those who have deliberately defected, we investigated if that defection could have been predicted by a poor Net Promoter Score or by any of the metrics in our own customer methodology.

The results were quite interesting. It transpired that a low 'Likelihood To Recommend' – the NPS question – was not the BEST predictor of customer defection but it was a pretty good one. Deep-Insight's own CRQ metric was a slightly better predictor while a low Commitment score – one of the key components of CRQ – was the best predictor of whether a B2B client was going to defect to the competition or not.

Whether we liked it or not, NPS did actually have a predictive capability for B2B organisations. It worked, not because NPS is the BEST predictor of whether a client was going to defect, but because it's a GOOD predictor, coupled with the fact that NPS has been embraced by some of the world's leading organisations as an easy-to-use and internationally-accepted customer benchmark. At Deep-Insight, we may have come a little late to the party – we only incorporated the Net Promoter Score into our customer methodology in early-2014 – and we have found the combination of NPS and our own CRQ metrics works well for our clients.

Net Promoter Score – Pros and Cons

Love it or loathe it, Net Promoter Score is now the de facto standard in customer feedback systems. Most customer experience (CX) programmes have NPS embedded into their fabric in some shape or form but it's worth noting a few things about NPS:

- It's one-dimensional (it is a single question, after all)
- It does struggle to cope with the complexities of a B2B environment
- It's also just a metric, not a framework for building customer-centric companies

In fairness to Fred Reichheld and Bain, they recognised that creating a customer-centric organisation required more than just a simple metric, so they rebranded NPS from Net Promoter Score to Net Promoter System and added a few additional concepts on leadership and communication to beef up the loyalty metric. Under communication, they advised companies to share the net promoter feedback with all employees that impacted the customer's experience of a particular product or service – the so-called *inner loop*. At the same time, companies need to act on the *outer loop* as well:

> Fred Reichheld: An outer loop must employ a rigorous, well-defined process for addressing issues. A team – usually led by the customer advocacy office, or CAO – gathers input from a variety of sources. That team uses clear and explicit criteria to prioritise opportunities for improvement. The CAO makes recommendations to senior executives about which opportunities to address and who should be accountable for leading the charge against each one. The assigned team then investigates root causes and develops solutions. Throughout the

process, the CAO makes sure that both customers and employees are informed about progress whenever doing so is relevant or required.

This discussion around the combination of the inner and outer loops is critically important for two reasons. First, it focuses attention on action rather than simply chasing a number. Second, it suggests a central function - the customer advocacy office or CAO – is required to act as the internal voice of the customer (VOC) in a company. That CAO function needs to have the ear of the CEO in order to make it effective. It certainly is not a low-level marketing function that commissions NPS research.

It was this closed loop analysis that helped BT's Gavin Patterson get real traction in terms of redesigning products and processes that were causing problems for customers.

Gavin Patterson: When we added the closed loop analysis of NPS to the operational metrics of Right First Time (RFT), that made a difference. I think NPS on its own is a little blunt, but the combination of NPS and the operational metrics around RFT is much more powerful. Hearing directly from customers makes a difference, and colleagues around the organisation are able to personalise failure in the process and personalise situations where we've let customers down. But in terms of providing diagnosis on an end-to-end basis for processes, it sometimes doesn't give the process designers and systems designers the currency they need to design failure out of processes and transaction time out of processes. So the combination of NPS and RFT seems to work for us and that's where, having initially flat-lined, we started to get some traction.

NPS Benchmarking

One further comment about NPS: if you are using it as a benchmarking and target-setting device, beware of published NPS benchmarks, particularly those scores you find on the Internet.

For starters, many of these scores are for B2C (business-to-consumer) companies and B2C responses tend to be very different to B2B scores. For example, well-known B2C brands can achieve very high NPS scores, particularly if the brand name is well-known and generally well-respected.

More important is the fact that NPS scores are notoriously subject to cultural differences and variations. Most of the companies featured in this book are European or Australian, while most of the published benchmark scores tend to be from American companies, and here's the rub. Americans score VERY differently to Europeans and Australians. In The Ultimate Question, Reichheld quotes NPS figures for well-known American brands that are primarily B2C.

Table 1 – Selected NPS Stars (Source: The Ultimate Question, Fred Reichheld)

USAA	82%	Intuit (TurboTax)	60%
HomeBanc	81%	Cisco	57%
Harley-Davidson	81%	Federal Express	56%
Costco	79%	Southwest Airlines	51%
Amazon	73%	American Express	50%
Chick-fil-A	72%	Commerce Bank	50%
eBay	71%	Dell	50%
Vanguard	70%	Adobe	48%
SAS	66%	Electronic Arts	48%
Apple	66%		

We don't know how Reichheld's scores were gathered and there are differences between email-based surveys and those that are conducted by telephone or in person. Telephone and face-to-face surveys tend to give much more positive results that email. As human beings, we generally don't like to give bad news and it's much easier to give bad news by email than face-to-face or even by telephone, so F2F and telephone scores tend to be inflated.

Similarly, there are significant differences in scores between surveys that are anonymous and those where the respondent knows that the surveyor will know his or her name. Non-anonymous surveys also have higher, artificially inflated scores.

In the B2B world, we find that an average NPS score in America might be in the region of +30 for an email-based anonymous survey. In Europe and Australia, an average score is in the region of +10. And there are significant differences across European countries as well. British and Northern European people tend to score much more harshly than their Eastern or southern European counterparts.

A Polish corporate banking client of ours has the ambition of being the best business bank in Poland. The recently recorded an NPS score of +70 and yet they have probably not yet achieved their goal as they know from external research that there are other banks with higher NPS scores in the market. On the other hand, a score of +40 in the UK or Germany would be seen as outstanding. Seriously, do be careful about benchmarking across international boundaries. We will return to this topic again in Part IV (Tactics & Execution) of this book.

Chapter 5 - A CX Framework

In the same way that Bain & Co extended the concept of Net Promoter from a 'score' to a 'system', senior executives need a much broader CX framework within which to look at customer-centricity. A combination of key performance indicators (KPIs) such as Net Promoter, Customer Satisfaction, Customer Effort or the myriad of other metrics that are currently in common usage, are certainly part of the answer as they provide different lenses through which to analyse the customer experience. However, there is a wider canvas to consider here, one that extends beyond the implementation of a set of customer metrics. The success of any customer experience programme involves the entire senior executive team and sales organisation but ultimately must go much further than that – it requires the buy-in from all parts of the organisation.

Metrics are one part of the solution but only a small part. To understand what needs to be done, a more all-encompassing framework is required and in this book we provide a framework for looking at the key elements that the executive team in any B2B company should address in order to become truly customer-centric.

Figure 6 – Framework for a Successful CX Programme

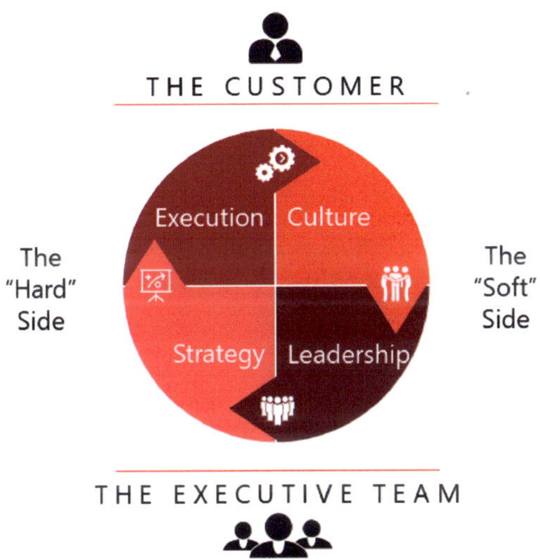

The framework essentially starts with the customer at the top of the model and the executive team as subservient. We then look at a series of tasks and activities that need to be carried out varying from 'hard' to 'soft' and as we'll see in this book, it is often the soft activities that tend to be overlooked or deprioritised.

The four elements are:

- Leadership
- Strategy
- Tactics & Execution
- Culture & Change

Leadership

Leadership is a 'soft quadrant' set of activities in that it can be difficult to monitor or apply metrics to. Yet, it is undoubtedly the most important of all the quadrants and leadership starts with the CEO. As we will see when we look at the case of Ursula Morgenstern, Joe Edwards and Atos UK & Ireland in more detail, if the CX programme is not driven by the CEO as a strategic priority, it is likely to fail. All the good examples of successful CX programmes that we have seen have been personally led by the CEO. If the CEO delegates the job to a CX director or sales director, the chances of it being a successful transformation are greatly diminished.

In Part II of this book (Leadership), we will examine the traits of successful customer-centred leaders:

1. They are genuinely passionate advocates for the customer
2. They take personal ownership of the customer agenda
3. They have an intuitive understanding that customer advocacy drives financial success
4. They use the customer agenda as a vehicle for change
5. They are relentless about Execution

Strategy

The role of the CEO or senior leadership team in any organisation is to set the tone for the company to become more customer-centric. However, the role extends much further. The same leadership team must craft decisions relating to customer segmentation, product portfolio and organisational design that will allow the customer to be placed at the heart of the company's strategy. Without these changes, the impediments will be too great and the overall CX programme will fail. As discussed earlier, it is simply not possible to be truly customer-centric if your clients are global and need a global account manager on their account, but the service provider is still siloed along country lines. Similarly, if a client is demanding a single point of contact but the company has six different product managers knocking on her door, that's not customer-centric.

Once these key decisions have been addressed, the next set of strategic decisions involve the establishment of a robust CX programme. Key elements that we discuss include:

- Business case
- Programme design
- Governance rules
- Metrics and KPIs

Tactics & Execution

Strategy without execution is just paper, as the saying goes. The best strategy in the world is useless unless there is an 'execution machine' in place to deliver on the CX strategy. In Part IV (Tactics & Execution) we explore the key elements of an execution strategy, including:

- Tactical Planning
- Executing the Plan
- Completing the Project
- Account Management

Culture & Change

Part V of this book (Culture & Change) involves another series of 'soft' activities that are important if the CX programme is to extend beyond the senior leadership team and become embedded into the DNA of the organisation. In our experience, the 'soft' activities of Leadership and Culture are the most challenging in CX programmes and often are the quadrants that are either under-resourced or, in some cases, completely ignored.

The keys to building the right CX culture are communication and empowerment – being very clear about what is expected from each part of the organisation but then allowing those parts of the organisation or those individuals to get on and take ownership of the CX programme.

A Tale of Two CX Transformation Journeys

All of the above messages are best summarised by way of a case study. Or two case studies – one successful; one less so. In truth there are many more CX programmes that fail to achieve their objectives than success stories.

Case Study – BT Ireland

Ten years ago, BT was a challenger telecommunications company in Ireland, having acquired a couple of local start-ups after the Irish telecommunications market had been deregulated. Over the next decade, BT Ireland moved strongly into the corporate market and eventually exited completely from the consumer market. It was a relatively small division of the larger BT Group and it was also unprofitable. When Chris Clark was dispatched from London to Dublin as the new MD, one of his first actions was to find out what his corporate customers thought of the company. The results were not good, but it provided Clark with a baseline understanding of what he needed to do to turn the company around.

The next six years were spent on a comprehensive transformation journey that can be divided into two parts. The first three years involved a re-engineering of the company's entire service model which Clark discovered was not fit for purpose, as well as a transformation of the sales and account management team under the leadership of a new sales director called Colm O'Neill. This period under Clark and O'Neill stabilised the company both in terms of operational capability as well as profitability. The journey from bad to good took three years. The underlying problems had now been fixed but BT Ireland was not yet truly customer-centric. The second period involved a different type of transformation: three years moving from good to great.

By this point, Chris Clark had returned to BT in London and Colm O'Neill was promoted to MD. O'Neill accelerated the pace of change. He appointed a CX Director called Mairead McSweeney who drove the programme with ruthless precision. We examine McSweeney's role in more detail in Part IV (Tactics & Execution) of this book. Customer scores were measured initially every six months and on an annual basis thereafter. Governance rules were put in place to ensure that the right individuals in the right clients were contacted for their views, and that the programme could not be 'gamed'. The entire organisation was incentivised on how well the customers scored BT Ireland. The sales teams had targets set either at an individual level or at a team level. The senior executive team had an overall BT Ireland target to hit for Customer Relationship Quality (CRQ) before incentives were paid out. O'Neill was personally involved throughout.

By the end of that second period – a total journey time of six years – BT Ireland was seen by its corporate customers as truly unique and its Net Promoter Score had moved from -40 at the beginning of its customer transformation to almost +25 at the end.

Figure 7 – The BT Ireland CX Journey

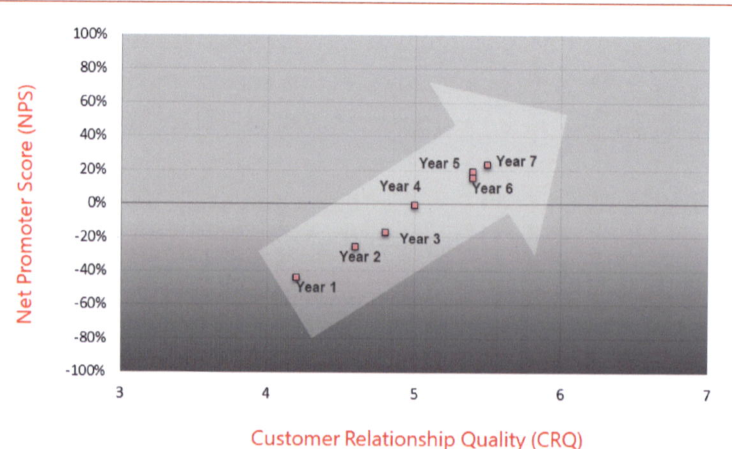

A few points are worth making about BT's customer experience transformation journey. First, it took time – years rather than quarters or months – and this is an important message for any CEO or CX Director. It's important not to under-estimate the length of time it takes to undertake a successful CX transformation. CX transformations are change programmes and change takes time. Second, it is equally important not to over-estimate what can be achieved if you get it right. BT Ireland went from a bottom decile customer score to a top decile score. It can be done. Third, although the scores on the graph appear almost too perfect, they are real, actual scores. At only one point during this journey did BT Ireland falter. Between Year 5 and Year 6, momentum stalled. Bonuses were not paid out because customer targets had not been achieved. The sense of deflation in the company were palpable. But the management team remained resolute. They redoubled their efforts and soldiered on.

Case Study – FINAX Europe (a pseudonym)

A second company that we have been working with closely for more than 5 years – we'll refer to them as FINAX Europe – provides back office services for the insurance industry. FINAX's clients are large European insurance companies and, as many large clients can be, are demanding. Our initial work with this company found that the underlying level of transactional service was poor. FINAX was not dissimilar to BT Ireland in that respect. There were multiple reasons for the poor underlying service and there was no silver bullet that could address the issues – if the root causes had been easy to identify, they would have been rectified long ago.

As is the case in many service delivery organisations, the underlying problem was a complex combination of old technology, poorly though-out processes that required significant manual intervention, combined with an internal culture where people worked hard but were anything but client-centred. The results were reflected in FINAX's customer scores – Net Promoter Scores that ranged from -40 to -70 during the years that we worked with them.

One example of the poor processes and manual intervention was the way orders were executed and processed by FINAX's back office teams. Every day, the back office would receive hundreds of instructions from clients by fax to be re-keyed into the company's own systems. As with all processes that require manual intervention, errors would occur. The error rate was actually relatively low but because of the large volumes of transactions, the absolute numbers or errors were actually quite high. And an individual error – such as entering a transaction for €1,000,000 instead of €100,000 – had serious repercussions.

One of FINAX's largest clients complained about a *"lack of robust processes"*. Another bemoaned a *"refusal to admit errors on their part and a culture of passing the blame"*. A third client summed it up as follows:

> FINAX just are not customer orientated and no matter how hard we try to reasonably engage with them towards getting a result, they keep letting us down. The harder we try, the more they take advantage. The stroppier we get, the more they build barriers. We just can't create a win-win with them! FINAX needs a stronger senior management team. As customers mature, their expectations of service quality increases and FINAX hasn't been able to meet expectations.

The senior management team in FINAX initially took these messages on board and set about trying to address the underlying issues. The problem with doing this is that the re-engineering of existing processes had to be carried out alongside the inevitable fire-fighting to rectify the errors that were occurring on a daily basis. What was required was an unwavering resolve to do whatever needed to be done to produce the best long-term results, no matter how difficult.

The problem was that this customer-centred leadership was missing. The CEO was not lacking in leadership capability and the company's strategic response was initially strong. However, the wider management team was weak and didn't have the resolve to see the programme through. FINAX also lacked the execution capability to set up and run a CX programme and execute it ruthlessly. They didn't have a Mairead McSweeney as BT Ireland had. FINAX's NPS score never rose above -30 and the board finally began to lose patience as the management team lost hope. Eventually, the CEO was removed and over the next few months, the new CEO replaced the entire senior management team in the organisation.

Summary of Part I

- B2C and B2B are very different. B2C is connecting intermittently with a large number of customers. B2B is developing and sustaining on-going and long-term relationships with a small number of key customers
- B2B customers, when analysed, can be categorised as ambassadors, rationals, ambivalents, stalkers and opponents
- B2B customer relationship quality is derived from three components – commitment, trust and satisfaction
- The value of being customer centric is well proven. It reflects in revenue, revenue growth and profitability over the long term
- Traditional companies are primarily product or service oriented, contemporary successful companies are primarily customer oriented
- The account manager is crucial to the quality of the customer relationship
- Various customer metrics exist – some are transactional (e.g. NPS), others are relationship focused
- A customer-centric framework must include leadership, strategy tactics & execution and culture & change

Part II – Leadership

Chapter 6 – Customer-Centred Leadership

- What Customer-Centred Leadership is Not
- The Art of Leadership

Chapter 7 – The Traits of Customer-Centred Leaders

Chapter 8 – Customer-Centred Leadership in Action

- Trait 1: Passionate Advocacy for the Customer
- Trait 2: Taking Personal Ownership of the Customer Agenda
- Trait 3: Intuitive Understanding that Customer Success drives Financial Success
- Trait 4: Using the Customer Agenda as a Vehicle for Change
- Trait 5: Being Relentless about Execution

Summary of Part II

"Great leaders are almost always great simplifiers who can cut through argument, debate, and doubt to offer a solution everybody can understand."

- Colin Powell

"Leadership is not magnetic personality that can just as well be a glib tongue. It is not 'making friends and influencing people'- that is flattery. Leadership is lifting a person's vision to high sights, the raising of a person's performance to a higher standard, the building of a personality beyond its normal limitations."

- Peter F. Drucker

"Good business leaders create a vision, articulate the vision, passionately own the vision, and relentlessly drive it to completion."

- Jack Welch

Chapter 6 - Customer-Centred Leadership

Many books have been written on the subject of leadership, and we do not intend this to become yet another book on the subject, so we will skim the surface on this topic. And yet leadership is important – the most important – element of becoming a customer centric company so it is a topic that warrants some attention.

Charles Handy is a management guru who worked with Shell International for a decade before moving into academia and writing about organisational behaviour. Few writers have been as influential as Charles Handy. His first book *Understanding Organisations* was published in 1976 when many readers of this book were not even born, but it has stood the test of time in terms of both writing style and freshness of content. The fourth chapter of the book is entitled *On Leadership* and it begins beautifully:

> Charles Handy: Leadership as a topic has rather a dated air about it. It smacks of trench warfare and imperial administration. It implies setting one person up above another, raises spectres of elites and privileged classes.

Handy goes on to ask a series of questions about the nature of leadership:

> Charles Handy: Is leadership, for the want of a better word, an innate characteristic? Are leaders born or made? Can anyone be a leader, or only the favoured few? Is there a particular trick to it or a particular style, something that, if we could learn it, would transform our lives? Are there models we should imitate, great ones that we can learn from?

Do you have to be popular to be effective? Or is it the other way round: is it impossible to be both well-liked and productive?

These are all good questions for which there are few clear-cut answers. Handy does his best to answer them by reviewing the literature on business leadership and summarising the results under three general headings: trait theories, style theories and contingency theories before concluding that:

Charles Handy: Each of these seems to contain some elements of truth but has always in the final analysis failed to explain enough of the difference between effective and ineffective leadership to be generally useful in a variety of situations. The theories will be discussed briefly and reviewed. A more complex, but potentially more realistic, model for understanding leadership situations will then be suggested and its implications discussed.

To use a sporting terminology, Handy kicks to touch here. He moves the subject on, having educated and put the reader in a better frame of mind to understand the topic, but ultimately leaves us a few metres short of the try line. In one sense, we are going to do the same in this book. We do not have a silver bullet for transforming your business into a truly customer-centric organisation but we will try – as Handy does – to provide you with a framework for understanding the key traits that customer-centred leaders have, and illustrate those with examples from interviews we have conducted with leaders who have managed to create customer-centric organisations.

What Customer-Centred Leadership is Not

Let's begin with an example of what Customer Centred Leadership is definitely NOT. How many times have you seen an announcement like this in the business news:

"ACME Europe is delighted to announce the appointment of a new Head of Customer Experience. This newly created role demonstrates ACME's commitment to its customers and ambition to become number one across Europe for customer service, trust and advocacy.

In a career spanning nearly 15 years, Winnie Dainsfort has gained a wealth of experience in the logistics industry and prior to joining ACME, having spent the last five years managing the European call centre functions at TransTrucking in Germany. Winnie has a Masters in Logistics Management from the University of Lyon and is a Six Sigma Black Belt in Lean Logistics.

Commenting on her appointment, Winnie said: 'I am delighted to take up this position and help drive the next phase of growth for ACME. It is truly a great honour to be joining a world class company like ACME.'

Winnie will report into Frederick Oberstein, ACME's Director of Service, who added: 'Our new customer strategy is based on putting the customer at the heart of everything we do. With Winnie on board, we are confident that we can continue delivering a world class service to our customers.'"

On the face of it, this is good news. ACME is investing in a newly created position to give the customer a much stronger voice at the table. What the announcement doesn't say is that the board of ACME removed the CEO six months earlier, after he had failed to stem losses for the second year running, and that the new CEO had been instructed to implement a customer experience programme based on a system called Net Promoter Score (NPS). Two of the board members had direct experience of using NPS in other companies and were insistent that a similar system be implemented in ACME. The new CEO delegated the task of hiring a CX manager to Fred Oberstein, and Fred duly hired Winnie into the new role.

Winnie is an experienced manager, knows how to manage customer service desks and had previously used NPS as a key performance metric in TransTrucking. She impressed Fred during the interview process and Fred was delighted to get her on board as his primary and overriding concern is fixing a service delivery function that he knows is fundamentally broken, as evidenced by the fact that ACME has failed to meet its DIFOT (Delivery In Full On Time) targets in all but two of the last 12 months and the opening of the new 20,000 sq. m. distribution centre in France is not operating at anything close to full capacity because of a series of teething problems. Fred needs Winnie to get the CX programme off the ground as he simply does not have the bandwidth to help her set up the programme, even if he had the skills to do so.

So, what are the chances of Winnie succeeding? The short answer is that we don't know but unless we can get some positive answers to the following questions, the answer might be 'less than 10%.'

So what questions would we ask? Here are a few for starters:

- Is the new CEO personally invested in this CX programme? Is she convinced that this is the right thing to do, or is she more focused on stemming the losses that caused her predecessor to be fired?
- Is her sales director also personally invested in the programme? After all, these are his customers and he owns the account teams that interface with the clients on a daily basis.

- What is the root cause of Fred's service delivery issue? Is it the French distribution centre or is it something more systemic in terms of poor processes or technology?
- What do ACME's largest customers really feel about their relationship with them, the service delivered and the company's ability to help them meet their own strategic objectives?

Winnie doesn't know the answers to all these questions but her first month in the role will help her gain some understanding of the key issues. She will then be in a better position to decide if she has made the right choice in moving to ACME and if the executive leadership team in ACME is capable of providing the direction, support and investment to make her CX programme work.

The Art of Leadership

In the above example, ACME is a fictitious company, but the thing is that ACME is representative of many companies that we have seen in the past. The press announcement is actually real – or at least is a combination of two real announcements that we have merged and sanitised in order to protect the innocent. As we saw in the case of FINAX, the delivery of excellent service on a consistent basis is not an easy trick to pull off, particularly in complex competitive industries where products and service offerings can change quickly. When there are serious underlying issues that require major interventions or significant investments, most leadership teams struggle to some degree or other. Even with a good leadership team in place, it takes a long time to effect change and turn poor customer relationships into robust long-lasting partnerships. This is a theme we will return to again and again in this book, particularly in Part IV (Tactics & Execution).

Customer-centred leadership is an art and cannot be vested in a single person. It requires a team approach and needs a performing group of dedicated, invested individuals who can complement each other and make things happen. But the role of the CEO or managing director is paramount so we should begin with the qualities that make for good executive leadership when the topic in question is nothing less than the transformation of the organisation into one that is truly customer-centric.

Jim Collins is an American author and lecturer who writes mainly on the subject of company sustainability and growth, but he has also delved into the question of what makes a truly great leader. One of the leadership concepts that Collins introduce was that of *Level 5 Leadership*. The concept stemmed from an analysis of 1,435 companies, of which Collins believed there were 11 truly great ones, and all were headed by Collins called 'Level 5 Leaders'. The leadership hierarchy is relatively straightforward:

- Level 1: Highly Capable Individual
- Level 2: Contributing Team Member
- Level 3: Competent Manager
- Level 4: Effective Leader
- Level 5: Great Leader

It's the characteristics of what Collins describes as Level 5 that are most interesting. Level 5 leaders have all of the abilities needed for the other four levels, plus you have the unique blend of humility and will that determine true greatness. Collins wrote about it in the Harvard Business Review and expanded on it in his book *Good to Great*, a management book that has sold more than 4 million copies to date.

Jim Collins: In Good to Great, as many of you know, we discovered the idea of the Level 5 leader, one blessed with a paradoxical blend of personal humility—that's the X factor of great leadership—personal humility with an utterly indomitable will. But the deep inner essence of Level 5 is the idea of service, of leading in service to a cause. We are talking here about ambition. Towering, exhausting, relentless, non-stop ambition, but channelled outward away from yourself into a cause, into an enterprise, into a purpose, into something that is bigger and more important than we are. See, ego-driven Level four leaders, they're really good at inspiring people to follow them. The Level 5 leaders inspire people to follow a cause. And therein is all the difference.

The 11 'Good to Great' companies – all Fortune 500 companies – are remarkable for the fact that nearly all of the great leaders of these companies are still relatively unknown, mainly because they made the journey from good to great about the company, and a vision of a company dedicated to service, rather than about themselves.

The journey from good to great doesn't happen overnight. And the transformation from good to great is resilient to change. It's enduring. One of Collins' Good to Great leaders Colman Mockler was CEO of Gillette from 1975 to 1991 (he died of a heart attack while in office) and the transformation of Gillette lasted the 16 years of his tenure but then continued after he died. A dollar invested in Gillette shares in 1976 was worth nearly €100 twenty years later.

Humility doesn't mean weakness. In Collins' view, Level 5 leaders demonstrate an *"unwavering resolve to do whatever must be done to produce the best long-term results, no matter how difficult"*. This concept is crucially important as change programmes of any kind take time. We have seen in Chapter 5 that the required unwavering resolve was missing in the case of FINAX's management team. The transformation of companies from being product-centric and internally-focused into world-class customer-centric organisations takes years and an unwavering resolve is a key requirement when shareholders demand results on a quarterly or 6-monthly basis.

Chapter 7 - Traits of Customer-Centred Leaders

From the analysis that we have done but more important, from the clients that we have worked with, it has become clear to us that the best customer-centred leaders are the ones who exhibit five key traits:

1. They are genuinely passionate advocates for the customer
2. They take personal ownership of the customer agenda
3. They have an intuitive understanding that customer success drives financial success
4. They use the customer agenda as a vehicle for change
5. They are relentless about Execution

Trait 1: Passionate Advocacy for the Customer

Leadership is all about setting the tone for others to follow. Enthusiasm and passion help to articulate the message. We will shortly examine how David Thodey demonstrated this passion for the customer when he was CEO of Telstra in Australia. We also see how Christine Corbett, the Chief Customer Officer of Australia Post was also a hugely enthusiastic advocate on behalf of her customers.

Trait 2: Taking Personal Ownership of the Customer Agenda

Passion and enthusiasm are fine, but more is needed. True leaders will lead from the front, rather than being figureheads. Ursula Morgenstern is a great example of leading from the front. When she found out that Atos's customers in the UK & Ireland were unhappy with the level, quality and consistency of service provided by Atos, she personally took ownership of the issue and created the 'Client At The Heart' programme that inspired the name of this book. Similarly, Colm O'Neill took personal ownership of the most challenging customer delivery issue that BT faced – the 'final mile' – when he took over as MD of its Major and Public Sector division. While O'Neill was taking on the 'final mile' issue, his Group CEO Gavin Patterson was also taking ownership of the customer agenda at the very top of the organisation by making customer feedback a regular discussion point at his leadership team meetings.

Trait 3: Intuitive Understanding that Customer Success drives Financial Success

In Australia, Telstra's David Thodey and Toll Group's Shane O'Neill both intuitively knew that improvements in customer satisfaction and customer advocacy would lead to improved financial performance. Telstra required Thodey to submit a business case to justify the CX programme while Toll simply accepted it as a fact that a radical transformation was needed. Regardless of whether a business case was required or not, both men had that intuitive understanding that greater customer advocacy would lead to increased profits.

Trait 4: Using the Customer Agenda as a Vehicle for Change

Winston Churchill is reported to have said *"Never let a good crisis go to waste."* Although he never actually said those words, they can be applied here as well. We will see in the next chapter how Colm O'Neill used the theme of 'Customer' as a rallying call for the change he wanted to implement in BT's Major and Public Sector division. David Thodey did exactly the same at Telstra.

Trait 5: Being Relentless about Execution

Leadership and Strategy are important but without a credible team and capability to execute that strategy, CX programmes are almost always doomed to under-deliver or to fail. In Atos and BT, the leadership teams made sure to put a strong execution capability in place and in both cases they were fortunate to find excellent execution skills and abilities in the form of Sue de Wit, Mairead McSweeney and Kathryn Whitehouse.

In the next chapter, we will examine these traits in more detail.

Chapter 8 – Customer-Centred Leadership in Action

Trait 1: Passionate Advocacy for the Customer

Telstra

Telstra is Australia's largest telecommunications company. David Thodey joined Telstra from IBM as the MD of its mobile division before moving to run its Enterprise and Government division the following year. When he became CEO of Telstra in May 2009 the company had 30,000 employees in Australia, a turnover of $25 billion and a terrible reputation for service. Thodey quickly announced a renewed focus on customer service and satisfaction. In an interview with the Australian Financial Review shortly after taking the CEO role, he was asked how he would want to be remembered.

David Thodey: I would like to be remembered as a CEO that made Telstra a company people were proud of, that Australians are proud of... that gave great customer service, that is a great place to work and that delivered great value to shareholders.

Thodey reiterated this message in Telstra's 2009 Annual Report – his first as CEO – by stating that Telstra's "strategy is to provide customers with world-class products and services to deliver a superior customer experience. While this is our strategy, we acknowledge not all experiences have yet met expectations. Our team is focused on quickly improving the customer experience so it becomes an unequivocal point of differentiation in the market place. Over the next 12 months a continued improvement in customer experience is a key priority for us".

When we interviewed David Thodey for this book, it became clear very quickly that even a decade after he took on the challenge of running Telstra, his passion for customer excellence had not dimmed and neither had the memories of the poor customer experience that were the hallmark of Telstra at the time.

David Thodey: When I became CEO, I used to get 60 complaint letters a day. Every day I was at Telstra, I read all 60 letters. Even when I was traveling overseas. And I put in place a rigorous process of acknowledging every complaint when it came in, and I signed every letter that went back out. I started doing it, and I didn't talk about it much. I should have talked about it earlier. Sometimes I might get a letter that was six pages long about some absolute service failure that would make you weep. But I would internalise it and use it as the energy to drive my passion to change things. As you can tell, I do get passionate about it.

Thodey went on to explain that his passion and drive was not simply focused on addressing and rectifying these customer service problems. It went much deeper than that. Thodey wanted to make Telstra truly customer-centric. He explained the difference between customer centricity and good customer service in the following fashion.

David Thodey: Customer centricity often gets confused with customer service, and yes, there are similarities, but customer centricity is far greater than just good customer service. When I ask people, “are you customer centric?” They say yes, but what they really mean is that they care about service. Customer centricity is far deeper.

I went to the Telstra board and I said “look, I think our strategy has got to be all about the customer and this company has become too internally focused. We've lost sight of who we really serve”. I said, “I want to put the customer as our core strategy" and they said "we want you to show us financially why it's a good idea to do that".

Customer centricity is greater than just customer service. It's around what you stand for, and it turns the company out to the outside. It creates a drive for change and reinvention. I've always wondered why companies lurch from transformation to transformation. If you really apply the voice of the customer to drive the change internally, you never arrive. You're always moving forward.

Putting the customer at the centre of Telstra's strategy was a personal commitment by David Thodey. It was not a glib statement made in Telstra's first annual report under his leadership, to be discarded in the following weeks or months. Thodey hitched both his own and Telstra's wagon to the promise of delivering better customer service to the customer and ultimately becoming a far more customer-centric organisation. It was this unwavering commitment and personal advocacy to the customer that helped turn around Telstra's fortunes in Australia.

Australia Post

Transforming product-centric and process-centric companies to customer-centric ones requires leadership and we have made the point that leadership must come from the very top. But large companies are not led by one individual alone. The wholehearted involvement of the executive team is also critical. Remember our FINAX case study from Chapter 5? Sometimes the CEO role needs to be supported through the creation of a role that gives the customers their own seat at the executive table.

Australia Post is a government-owned enterprise that provides postal services locally and internationally. On 1 July 2017, Australia Post appointed it first ever Chief Customer Officer: Christine Corbett. Corbett's portfolio covered brand, marketing and community engagement, as well as the customer experience (CX) function. When we interviewed her for this book, we asked her why the role was created.

Christine Corbett: When we introduced the Chief Customer Office, the decision was led by both the board and the CEO. We had just come out of the postal reform process where there were significant changes and we needed to win both the hearts and minds of our customers. The creation of a Chief Customer Officer position was to focus on customers across all business units and to reposition Australia Post externally. We needed to know what it was that customers wanted and expected from Australia Post.

Part of my role was to be the customer advocate in the room. There needed to be a different discussion and debate and we needed to be more deliberate in understanding what the impact of decisions would be on our customers. That was the change around the board and executive table.

Trait 2: Taking Personal Ownership of the Customer Agenda

Atos UK & Ireland

Atos is a European IT services firm and one of the world's top 20 IT consultancy companies. The current Atos organisation is the result of a series of mergers, including the acquisition of KPMG Consulting in 2002 and SchlumbergerSema in 2004. One of the largest deals was the acquisition of the IT services subsidiary of German engineering firm

Siemens in 2011, which doubled the size of the company to 74,000 employees and annual revenues of nearly €7 billion.

Shortly after the Siemens deal, Ursula Morgenstern took over the role of CEO at Atos's UK & Ireland division, with Joe Edwards as her sales and marketing director. The Atos story is one about leadership in action and how a customer centric culture can be driven from the top down, by the senior leaders taking personal ownership of the programme.

Following the Siemens deal, Atos UK & Ireland had almost 10,000 staff and Joe Edwards' task was to deliver annual revenues of nearly £1 billion from an enlarged customer base. He decided to get feedback from Atos' largest government and private sector clients in a more formal and structured fashion that had been done in the past. Edwards was expecting some negative feedback – although the company was doing well in securing new contracts in the marketplace, it was finding it more difficult to win new business from existing clients. Joe knew something wasn't quite right, but he didn't have enough evidence to identify what the issues really were and what needed to be done to address them. In April 2012, he found out.

Joe Edwards: If I'm perfectly honest, when we saw the first set of customer research results, we were shocked. We thought they weren't going to be very good, but we were shocked that they were as bad as they were. That was a disappointment, and we had to get over that and say this is what our customers are telling us, and we are either going to do something about this or we're not.

Then, if you're going to go down the line of seeking feedback from the client through a research process, then by God, you'd better do something with it, because the worst thing you can do is stimulate a client to think that you are going to do something and then don't. That's worse than doing nothing.

I don't think our CEO Ursula Morgenstern had any real view of how good or bad things were, and when she saw this, she really got in behind me and said, "You know what? We really are going to have to change this. We really are going to have to do something differently" and that involved, in some instances, changes of people. In other instances, investment in particular sectors and accounts. It involved a more rigorous approach to account planning and it suddenly got people's attention.

This was a chief executive's issue, and she took responsibility. I helped her shine the light on it, and she was incredibly supportive of what I was doing, but she then took the responsibility and said, "I'm really going to drive this hard so that we get an improvement in these accounts". The responsibility for a programme like that has to belong to the CEO.

Joe is a tall, imposing sales director and not lacking in self-confidence. But he makes an interesting point when he talks about who needs to take leadership for a Customer Experience (CX) programme. As sales director, it was Joe's job that was on the line if customers weren't happy and failed to renew contracts. Many people feel that a CX programme in a B2B organisation needs to be driven by the sales director and although Joe wouldn't disagree with that, he is also clear that the leadership and direction for a company-wide CX programme – particularly one that requires significant change to be made – requires leadership and personal involvement from the CEO.

Indeed, it was Morgenstern who kicked off an initiative called Client At The Heart. Morgenstern took personal ownership of the programme even if the day to day execution of the programme was carried out by a small team led by Sue de Wit. Sue joined Atos in 2010 through the acquisition of Siemens and, as the new Head of Client Experience, Sue describes how she and Joe Edwards set about addressing customer issues in a more systematic way under Ursula Morgenstern's guidance.

Sue de Wit: People copy behaviours and people will follow leaders and leaders need to set the example in terms of where the focus needs to be. In that first year, there's still far too much focus on internal issues, or just minor tweaks. So, Client At The Heart really came about with Ursula saying "right, we need a theme, we need to be customer centric as an organisation so what is the message that we can put out there?" And we were very successful by making sure that a whole campaign was put around it. We didn't really know right at the beginning with Client At The Heart exactly what we were going to do, we just knew we wanted to be more customer-centric.

Client At The Heart really came after realising you can't do this in small, piecemeal bits. You really need executive sponsorship. And in our case, we're lucky that we had the CEO saying: "This is my Number 1 priority, to be a customer centric organisation; it's my programme of work to address it and I'm going to call it Client At The Heart and it's not just about improvement plans."

There was so much more around it at the time, in terms of Ursula doing all-employee calls where she would make it her number one thing to talk about in terms of her Client At The Heart update. And it could just be "I've been to see this customer, and this customer, and we're doing some fantastic things for them." Not all necessarily related to improvement activity but just to say "the customer is THE most important thing to me".

Edwards agrees that the customer agenda must be sponsored at the highest level within the organisation.

Joe Edwards: It is top down. The CEO has to commit personal time to really drive the programme that you put in place. The CEO can't delegate it to someone else. It has to be their responsibility if you are going to get the buy-in of both your own organisation and the clients whose service you are seeking to improve.

BT

BT Group is a British telecommunications company which trades under the BT (formerly British Telecom) and EE brands in the United Kingdom. It has operations in 180 countries although the UK remains its core market.

Colm O'Neill took on the role as MD of the Major and Public Sector (MPS) division of BT in 2015, having previously run BT's Irish operations. Over the previous five years, the BT Ireland team had built a tremendous reputation for customer centricity but O'Neill knew that his new expanded role in the UK would be more challenging. BT's MPS division was a complex business that encompassed all of the company's large government clients – local police forces, government departments, the National Health Service – but also several thousand private sector accounts, all with different needs and agendas.

For years, MPS had been plagued by service delivery problems and O'Neill knew that he had to lead from the front. He couldn't just leave it to the sales teams and expect them to deliver all the change. The one area he picked to lead on was probably the most challenging customer delivery issue that BT faced – the 'final mile.' The final mile is a phrase widely used in the telecommunications industry to describe the final leg in the journey to deliver a service to a business customer. Very often it requires laying new cables to a building which requires working with local councils and businesses to get permission to dig up streets, lay cables, and bring that service into the client's premises. In the UK, that work is done by a company called Openreach which also happens to be part of the BT Group. (Openreach provides these engineering services to all telecommunications providers in the UK, not just BT.)

Colm O'Neill: I publicly said to our team, "What I want you to do is to own this survey process and own improving our service. Get to our customers, get them to engage in the survey process and promise to Fix One Thing at each client. My commitment is that I will personally own our biggest problem, which is 'Final Mile' delivery." Our biggest customer satisfaction issue was delivery of the 'final mile' service. This was provided by a regulated company within the BT Group and so we had very clear and explicit regulated rules of engagement.

So we built a dedicated team of people to fix this 'final mile' delivery issue in our business. It became very clear that more than half of the issues were caused by how we were interacting with this regulated business unit. So, we worked really collaboratively with them, within the boundaries of the regulatory system. We fixed all the things we could fix. They started to fix the things they could fix. We had a huge step forward in service delivery.

In one of our first customer surveys we had adverse comments of 30% referring to 'final mile' delivery. In our most recent survey, it's less than 4%. That gained great credibility with our team because they started to believe that we were serious about tackling the big issues and they had people who were behind them. It built belief and on that belief we've continued to build momentum. We've taken a massive step forward last year.

Keeping customer experience and the programme supporting it alive and current in the business is a challenge. You need to ensure that its not kicked down the road till it is too late to do anything to improve the survey score. You need to build momentum early.

O'Neill makes it sound easy. It wasn't, and he knew that if he didn't take personal ownership of what was the greatest source of frustration to BT's customers, then little was going to happen with the overall CX programme. While O'Neill was dealing with the Openreach 'final mile' issue in his division, his Group CEO Gavin Patterson was also taking ownership of the customer agenda by weaving the voice of the customer into the fabric of his Executive Committee (ExCo) meetings.

Gavin Patterson: I made sure that as an ExCo, we spent a lot of time working on customer issues together. So every two weeks we look at an extensive dashboard of metrics by line of business and each line of business was designed around a customer's need. And through closed loop feedback on both NPS and RFT (Right First Time), we reviewed as a group where we are against our objectives. We had limited traction for the first couple of years but in the last three and a half years we've seen consistent quarter on quarter improvement in all those measures. And what I've noticed is, because it is on the ExCo agenda and we're reviewing it every two weeks, it sets a real tempo in the organisation.

As part of taking ownership for the customer agenda, Patterson also did what David Thodey did at Telstra – he insisted on hearing first hand from the customer how they felt about BT, its products and its processes. Warts and all.

Gavin Patterson: You have to have an unfiltered stream of customer data, and by that I mean as CEO things are often prepared for you, filtered and beautifully packaged and presented. And that's good but you also have to complement it with direct access to customer data

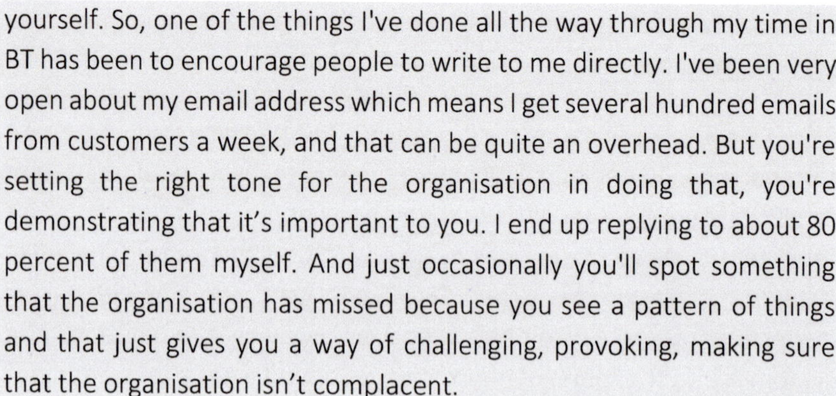

yourself. So, one of the things I've done all the way through my time in BT has been to encourage people to write to me directly. I've been very open about my email address which means I get several hundred emails from customers a week, and that can be quite an overhead. But you're setting the right tone for the organisation in doing that, you're demonstrating that it's important to you. I end up replying to about 80 percent of them myself. And just occasionally you'll spot something that the organisation has missed because you see a pattern of things and that just gives you a way of challenging, provoking, making sure that the organisation isn't complacent.

Trait 3: Intuitive Understanding that Customer Success drives Financial Success

Telstra

David Thodey's passion to improve the customer experience for Telstra's customers and to be 'an agent for the customer' was genuine but was also grounded in a hard-nosed commercial belief that a truly customer-centric organisation would deliver superior returns for shareholders in the long run.

Ultimately, the market decides whether customer centricity delivers results. Thodey led Telstra for six years between 2009 and 2015 and by the time he left, the company was in much better financial health than when he took over the reins as CEO.

David Thodey: Our EBITDA improved by 35%. Our share price started at \$3.20, then when I become CEO it dropped to \$2.60 but we finished at \$6.50. We had doubled the valuation of the company. Morale went up and every metric went up. Employee engagement was up in the eighties, which was the highest we had ever had.

David Thodey had an intuitive understanding that customer centricity would lead to financial success. However, he still had to build a business case for the investment required to make customer centricity a reality in Telstra.

David Thodey: We had to do a big business case and it was really interesting, because rather than just being a nice sentiment or a worthy ideal, we had to go through a detailed analysis of the benefits of being customer centric - so it was good for the shareholders.

We based the business case on reduction of churn (loss of customers) and the lifetime value of the customer including the propensity of the customers to buy multiple products.

Then we realised that we didn't have the systems in place to measure how customers perceived us, how they reacted, so we invested sixty million dollars in making it happen. I wouldn't want your readers to get put off by that number because $60 million to Telstra is not a lot of money when you've got a $24 billion company. We had to put in a set of rigorous processes that would measure interactions, product satisfaction, process satisfaction, and make the data available in real time.

Toll Group

Other companies don't require a business case – they just accept the fact that financial success will follow greater customer advocacy. Here's the view from Shane O'Neill, a divisional director at Toll Global Express, part of Toll Group, an iconic brand in Australia. Toll has 40,000 employees providing transport and logistics services by road, air, sea and rail not just in Australia but in more than 50 countries across the globe.

Shane O'Neill: We determined that we didn't need a business case for our investment in this process. Our new CEO recognised that we were getting bad press in terms of our customer forums, on social media, and from the 'larger end of town' in terms of feedback. We were getting this from our contacts and from the large contracts that we were losing. Obviously, we knew we had a problem and we knew we needed to change it.

We started off with a light touch by investing in customer surveys. In typical Toll fashion, there were different methodologies adopted across different divisions. At least we were now actually trying to understand how big or how small the problem was. Before then it was anecdotal, it was intuition, or it was just ignored. Now, we took a proactive step to get feedback, measure where the problem was, and then start to look at how we could actually fix it.

It was being done in a division-by-division level, then we brought it together under a corporate umbrella. We used Net Promoter Score (NPS) and we focused on the top 20 or 50 customers for NPS and in-depth interviews. Some of the stuff that came out was quite heartening for those customers where they had a good relationship with their account manager, they were getting great service, et cetera, to downright damning from where customers who were getting crap service and had a very poor strategic relationship.

BT Ireland

Earlier in this chapter, we quoted Colm O'Neill, the CEO of BT's Major and Public Sector division, who had previously run the Ireland division for the UK-headquartered telecommunications company.

In 2009, O'Neill was hired by MD Chris Clark from the American technology company EMC as BT Ireland's sales director. As we discussed earlier, the Irish operations represented a small part of BT's revenues and was not profitable. O'Neill and Clark shared the same innate belief that happy customers mean excellent financial performance, and both were fully behind a nascent customer experience programme that Clark had started in order to transform the company's fortunes. When O'Neill took over the MD role in 2011, he accelerated the efforts to put trusted customer relationships at the very heart of the company's strategy. And that strategy paid dividends (literally – to the parent company) as O'Neill describes:

Colm O'Neill: We experienced a massive improvement and step forward in customer experience in the BT Ireland business, we've completely turned that business around financially and operationally. The Republic of Ireland business is very highly regarded within the BT Group and recognised as one of the top performing businesses globally by every metric. The Northern Ireland business, which is part of the UK, is also considered a benchmark business within the group by every measure.

Along with customer experience success came enormous financial success. You can plot improvement in customer experience alongside financial performance and there is an undeniable direct correlation. Every time you go through those changes you get an increase in confidence in the philosophy that if you make an organisation a customer focused organisation, you will deliver great financial performance.

Whether the board or CEO requires a business case to be built or not, the key trait here is the innate belief that customer success and financial success are linked.

Trait 4: Using the Customer Agenda as a Vehicle for Change

Trait 4 is in many ways an extension of Trait 3. If you know that being customer-centric is a sensible financial move, why not use it to justify and fund a wider change programme? We pick up the story again from BT's Colm O'Neill.

BT Major and Public Sector

When O'Neill moved from Ireland to run BT's Major and Public Sector (MPS) division in 2015, the company was at an inflection point in its history. The acquisition of the mobile operator EE had been announced earlier that year but not yet approved by the regulators. This would be a transformational move by BT as it would bring them back into the mobile business in the UK, having floated off its O2 mobile division a decade earlier. The EE integration into BT also promised to be hugely challenging as EE was itself a joint venture formed by crashing together Deutsche Telecom's T-Mobile and France Telecom's Orange UK businesses. Both were sub-scale in the UK market but the merger allowed EE to eliminate management roles and back office functions and amalgamate high street locations, thus creating a more powerful and financially stable brand. Several thousand jobs were lost as a result of the merger and now EE was going to go through a second, more significant integration process. O'Neill picks up the story:

Colm O'Neill: The BT UK role involved a highly complex scenario where BT was acquiring EE and we were doing an internal merger of another two internal business units.

The internal business we were merging in was in a lot of financial distress and was part of a profit warning for BT. We had important things to do initially around baselining the financials and making sure we could help the board and the market understand what the underpinning dynamics were - what was happening and what our strategy was.

I was looking for something that could be a uniting principle for these diverse groups of people in this complicated situation. Customer experience was a banner I felt everyone could identify with and march forward with the business. I also believed that if we could make improvements here there would be a direct impact on reducing our costs and improving out margins, particularly through renewal cycles.

Even though we weren't doing a particularly good job of delivering customer service, one of the things you found with BT people was that they were true customer advocates, just not always equipped to deliver on that advocacy. They wanted to be doing a great job.

I took a bit of a risk because I convincing our stakeholders, which included the board of the company, that customer experience would be the thing that would lead us out of this, but it was not straightforward. There was a clear financial plan that underpinned it and they were very supportive. It was a clear strategy but it would be judged by its successful delivery of improved financial performance.

It is worth noting that the overall BT environment was also shifting its focus in this direction. One of the first things Gavin Patterson said when he took the reins as Group CEO was, on his watch, he was going to look to address the service issue in BT right across the board.

EMC

The same story happened at EMC, an American technology company that has since merged with Dell. You will recall that Colm O'Neill had been the country MD for Ireland at EMC prior to moving to BT. At the time, EMC was a small company selling computer disc arrays, or storage devices, to companies with large complex needs.

Colm O'Neill: At the time, EMC was trying to carve out a little segment in the market place, and they actually had quite a poor reputation from a customer satisfaction perspective, because they were putting their disc arrays into environments where little problems used to occur. They were selling these commodities into the middle of complex environments, and they didn't have a particularly good service reputation when they started out.

When I was at EMC, I remember the CEO at the time Mike Ruettgers decided to put a new guy called Frank Hauck into the customer service role to fix all these issues. He came up with a simple one-liner to embody what he felt the company needed to do to become brilliant at customer service. It was 'Guilty Until Proven Innocent.' He said, "When there's any problem in the environment, we're going to be guilty until we can absolutely prove we're innocent."

That kicked off a philosophy on service and developed to the point where EMC built an Interoperability Lab. It dealt with anything that would plug into the EMC environment. If we introduced a new software patch or a new piece of hardware it would go through the full interoperability testing in EMC before we would accredit it. Then the whole service ethos and engineering processes were built around that one sentence 'Guilty Until Proven Innocent.' It was a rallying point.

Telstra

David Thodey says the same about his time at Telstra, and how the voice of the customer can be used as a powerful lever in driving innovation through the company.

David Thodey: I think the principle of using the voice of the customer, or the market, to drive change, and really instilling it so that it's in every conversation, is incredibly powerful. It drives innovation, and re-invention. You're in this constant mode of creating a learning organisation.

Trait 5. Being Relentless about Execution

Some years back, Ram Charan wrote a management book called *Execution: The Discipline of Getting Things Done* with American CEO and turnaround expert Larry Bossidy. The main premise behind the book is that the real job of leadership is not about formulating a vision for the company and leaving others to implement it. Bossidy believes that true leaders must be engaged deeply and passionately in managing the organisation and that success requires a discipline in execution: understanding how to link together people, strategy, and operations, the three core processes of every business.

Charan and Bossidy give many examples of companies that have had excellent visions and strategies, but only some have succeeded while others have failed. The difference between success and failure is down to the quality of the leadership teams in orchestrating those three core processes of hiring the right people, building a strategy that's in sync with the marketplace and the competition, and an operating process that is built on clear actions and accountability.

BT Group

At BT Ireland, Colm O'Neill was lucky to have a talented team working for him. O'Neill describes himself as an ideas man, but he appreciated the need to have a strong execution capability.

Colm O'Neill: I like ideas. I like generating ideas and thoughts and discussing things. My core default style is not execution, but it has been at the centre of everything I've done in my career because I just know the value of it. That's why you also need a core person who is an 'execution machine'. You give them the problem, and they divide it up into all the bits and get them done.

I fully believed that this was important, and I was supported by the chief executive at the time. After that, what's important are incentives, focus, and execution.

The focus and execution were provided by Mairead McSweeney. She and O'Neill had an excellent working relationship built on a strong mutual respect for each other's capabilities. We'll spend more time in the Tactics & Execution part of this book looking at how McSweeney took O'Neill's ideas and turned them into actions but for the purposes of this chapter, we will just recall Mairead's first encounter with her new Managing Director.

Mairead McSweeney: I remember when Colm became MD of BT Ireland and I had my first meeting with him, and he just said, "Let there be no misunderstanding: you are accountable for this." So, I thought, right, this man is going to drive me to succeed. And he did.

Several years later, when O'Neill moved to the UK to head up BT's Major and Public Sector division, he enrolled another 'execution machine' into his team – Kathryn Whitehouse. O'Neill's initial message to Whitehouse was remarkably similar to the conversation he had with McSweeney.

Kathryn Whitehouse: Colm said to me: "No pressure but this is going to be the most important thing that we do as an organisation. I absolutely think that our success is going to make, or break, based on how we develop this process, how we engage with our customers and how we use the customer experience process as a way of jointly or collaboratively measuring our success and our progress with our customers."

Relentlessness about execution is also a requirement at the most senior levels of an organisation, if customer centricity is become a reality. In many situations, CX programmes will stall or fail to gain traction and in such cases the CEO needs a combination of resilience and relentlessness to ensure that traction is gained, momentum built and results delivered. Gavin Patterson describes the situation at BT when, 18 months into his CEO tenure, that traction and momentum were proving difficult to achieve.

Gavin Patterson: After the first 18 months as CEO and not feeling as though we were making any progress, that was the moment when my leadership was tested the most from a customer perspective. I could feel people's enthusiasm begin to wane, the board were frustrated with progress, and you feel as though there are times when you simply don't understand why it isn't responding. It's those sorts of dark moments where you've got to ensure the people keep the faith, and you continue to work on what the issue is until you begin to get traction. That's the most testing time for leadership and often that's the CEO's moment, when they are the ones that have to believe when everybody else around them is beginning to give up.

I think for me it was getting the combination of metrics right and the cadence. Cadence is all about tempo. Tempo sets priority. It gives people a sense of priority. We had a cadence of bi-weekly reviews and that made a difference. I look back and think if I had realised that right at the beginning, I would have shortened the time it took us to gain traction.

Atos UK & Ireland

In the same way that Colm O'Neill had an execution machine in Mairead McSweeney and later in Kathryn Whitehouse, Ursula Morgenstern's equivalent in Atos UK & Ireland was her Head of Client Experience Sue de Wit. Sue's role was to help shape and execute the vision that Ursula and her sales director Joe Edwards were creating.

Sue de Wit: When I took a sales operations role there was very little focus on customer satisfaction. It coincided with Joe and Ursula wanting to put focus on it so it was the ideal opportunity to say, "Right, let's take stock and look across the client base of old teams, and old customers and see where we are." And that's when we first started working together and we looked at that across the piece, and that 2012 client assessment was really the initial shocking one.

It was at that point that the 'Client At The Heart' programme got born. Ursula and Joe both had that real focus of saying, "We need to put the customer lens on all of these decisions." We had an initial customer insights survey which gave us a baseline and then we left it to the individual accounts to try and make a difference in that first year. Then of course, when we had the second set of results, there were some accounts that had managed to make an improvement, but it just wasn't at all what we were looking for. We came to the natural conclusion that people copy behaviours and people will follow leaders and leaders need to set the example in terms of where the focus needs to be. In that first year there was still far too much focus on internal issues, or just minor tweaks and people wanting to do it their own way.

We will pick up these themes in the next two parts of this book when we look at the importance of creating the right customer strategy and then executing that strategy in a clear and compelling way.

Summary of Part II

- An organisation seeking customer centricity must have a customer-centric leader
- The traits of customer-centric leaders are:
  - They are genuinely passionate advocates for the customer
  - They take personal ownership of the customer agenda
  - They have an intuitive understanding that customer success drives financial success
  - They use the customer agenda as a vehicle for change
  - They are relentless about execution

Part III - Strategy

Chapter 9 – Three Pillars of a Customer-Centric Strategy

- The Customer Component
- The Product Component
- The Organisational Component

Chapter 10 – Why Strategy is Important

- How do 'Strategy' and 'Tactics' Relate
- Are we selling Products or Servicing Customers?
- Competitive Positioning
- B2B2C and B2B2B
- Trust
- Gaining Commitment
- Corporate Values
- Project Management Methodology

Chapter 11 - Business Case

- Writing the Business Case
- Rewards & Recognition Strategy
- Contents of a Business Case
- Return on Investment (ROI)
- Example Business Case

Summary of Part III

"A vision without a strategy remains an illusion."

- Lee Bolman

"Strategy is about setting yourself apart from the competition. It's not a matter of being better at what you do – it's a matter of being different at what you do."

- Michael Porter

"Hope is not a strategy."

- Vince Lombardi

Chapter 9 – Three Pillars of a Customer-Centric Strategy

Vince Lombardi was a famous American football coach who took over a completely dispirited Green Bay Packers team in 1959 and led them to three consecutive NFL Championships in 1965, 1966 and 1967 followed by victory in first two Superbowl championships in 1967 and 1968.

Lombardi is reputed to have said *"hope is not a strategy"* but the origins the of the phrase are a little vague. If Lombardi was not the first person to use these five words, the movie director James Cameron certainly did use the following lines at a NASA symposium in 2004: *"Luck is not a factor. Hope is not a strategy. Fear is not an option."* The context of his talk was the logistical preparations for the movie Titanic and more specifically, the diving expedition to the site of the wreck 4,000m below the surface of the North Atlantic.

James Cameron: When I started our most recent expedition project, I called a big summit meeting of all the department heads. I stood in front of a white board and put up on the white board three slogans. The slogans were there: "Luck is not a factor", "Hope is not a strategy", "Fear is not an option". Now the first two were meant to convey my philosophy that to succeed in any complex task, it is essential to leave nothing to chance. You need to make your own luck by rigorous application of a robust process. You test everything in a very disciplined fashion, you don't guess, you know the answer, you anticipate every negative condition that might possibly prevail. You assume it is going to happen. You have an A plan, a B plan, a C plan, and you assume that you're going to be on the C plan by your second cup of coffee on morning one of the expedition, because that's how it goes when you're at sea.

This chapter is also about logistical preparation, but for running a comprehensive customer experience (CX) programme rather than for managing a successful sports team or a complex diving expedition. Even so, many of the same principles about robust processes, rigorous testing, dedication and discipline still apply.

The specific components of strategy that are key to building a customer-centric organisation are:

1) The Customer component;

2) The Product component;

3) The Organisational component.

Any senior executive planning a journey towards customer-centricity must be extremely clear about their approach in each of these three strategic areas.

The Customer Component

The starting point of any customer centricity strategy is a clear understanding of the type of customers the company want to serve. This is important. Leadership teams must be crystal clear about what an 'ideal' customer looks like and why their set of products, services and offerings will meet the needs of that ideal customer better than those of the competitors. Cynergy Bank is a specialist business bank in the UK with a very clear view that its ideal customer is a small to medium sized enterprise (SME) and specifically the 'M' customer that currently is not particularly well-served by the larger British banks like HSBC and Barclays. Cynergy does not want to be all things to all people.

It wants to stay focused on the niche where it knows it can do well and where its products and approach to relationship management can win. It measures the success of its strategy through the Net Promoter Score (NPS) metric.

Leadership teams also need clarity around how they are going to segment their customers. In most B2B organisations, the Pareto rule applies where 80 percent of revenues comes from 20 percent of clients. Larger strategic customers do need to be treated differently to the others. Strategic customers do not even need to be the largest. Some customers have relatively small revenues but significant potential. These companies are also strategic and good customer segmentation is rarely done solely on revenues but typically on potential as well.

In Chapter 2, we stated that one of the most fundamental strategic decisions a company can make in its journey towards customer-centricity is the segmentation of its clients. The reason that it's important to have a clear agreed approach to segmentation is that it drives much of the account management strategy and often the operational strategy needed to service those customers. We started that discussion with the story of Joe Edwards, an account executive at HP with 10 or 15 accounts to manage, who suddenly finds out that his entire world was about to be changed when his boss decided to refocus the company's efforts on a smaller number of key clients, and Edwards' portfolio was reduced from 10-15 down to a single client: Boots.

Joe Edwards: I had to understand what Boots was all about as a business, and that meant spending a lot of time on-site to the point where I spent about three days a week with them. I used to hold clinics in the canteen and anyone who was about who had an IT problem would come and see me. Bit by bit, I built up a set of relationships and trust that convinced them that I wasn't just in it for taking the order, but I was in it for the long term. I was trying to improve service and the relationship between the two companies for mutual benefit.

I learned a lot about account planning from the perspective of getting further penetration into the client company. I didn't know enough about the supply chain or stock room in Boots which we had some opportunity in. I needed to understand the customer from a business perspective, not just from an IT point of view.

The lesson I took from it was 'the plan'. If you don't have a plan, you're going nowhere. If you don't create 'customer intimacy' in the sense of understanding what your client is, what market they're playing in, and what new things you can bring to the client to excite them on a regular basis. If you're not bringing anything to the table, and therefore the relationship starts to decline.

The message that not all customers should be treated equally might sound at odds with the title of this book. We are not saying that some customers should be treated well and others badly. We are saying that all customer segments should be treated appropriately.

Not all clients need or want a dedicated account manager. In some cases, a dedicated telephone-based service team can do a more cost-effective - and sometimes a better - job than an account manager on the road. It might sound like a customer is being given a lower level or service but the standardisation of service though a well-managed desk-based team can provide a more appropriate and consistent service for smaller clients.

When we did some work at Irish Life, the largest life assurance company in Ireland, we found that the smaller brokers who sold Irish Life's products were managed by a telephone-based service team had better broker relationship scores than many of the larger brokers with named relationship managers. Some of this was because the smaller brokers had different – and lower – service needs and expectations but the main reason was that the service team was properly resourced, well-managed and had well-designed processes for handling the majority of broker queries. Most insurance companies adopt a similar model.

QBE is a large insurance provider in Australia. Its larger brokers have a named broker relationship manager and these BRMs are organised along state lines and visit their brokers regularly. QBE's smaller brokers are all handled by a small dedicated support team based in Paramatta in New South Wales, where all broker contact is via the phone and internet.

The Product Component

The second key component of strategy relates to the products and services that companies sell to their customers. Too often, companies have either the wrong product offering or an incoherent range of products and services for their clients. Very often this is an organic development: a company launches a new product range but does not retire an existing product; a new company is acquired but the combined product range is not rationalised.

Old products that are not retired tend to linger on in a no man's land where they are not actively marketed but continue to provide a drain on the company's cost base. Most products have some 'cost of ownership' in that they require certain tools to manufacture them, certain raw materials to be kept in stock, or certain software systems, processes and 'know how' to support and maintain them. These is also another hidden cost – the impact that an unwieldy product range has on customer satisfaction. Timico is a technology company that supports the IT needs of over 15,000 clients from three locations in the UK. It has grown by acquisition since in was founded 15 years ago. According to its customers, one of its greatest strengths is its wide product range but that has also become a major challenge in terms of the company's ability to maintain and support such a wide range of technology offerings. Timico management have recently embarked on a project to rationalise the product range with the objective of simplifying processes and improving customer service and support.

Traditional companies can often get away with a large or incoherent product range but in the digital world, competition tends to be more fierce and the use of customer data to inform product decisions is more critical. Our interview with eBay's Eamonn Galvin was enlightening in this regard.

Eamonn Galvin: There are two parts to my career. During the early part of my career at Accenture, I worked with companies like Ericsson and Microsoft, before moving into operating roles with General Electric on a very data-driven role and then moved to eBay in late-2008. That's when I first started to use net promoter score (NPS). The context was European. eBay was a very strong platform particularly in the UK and Germany, but under significant pressure from Amazon.

This battle with Amazon gave Galvin some key insights into how product strategy in the online world must be informed constantly by customer feedback, particularly when it comes to making key decisions about product investments. When Galvin joined eBay, the company was competing with Amazon in similar spaces. Although we tend to think of both companies as having consumer offerings, they are in fact B2B2C firms with eBay generating a significant proportion of its revenues from goods sold online by small businesses rather than individuals.

Like Amazon, eBay's primary product is its marketplace platform. Its challenge – and Amazon's – was to make its marketplace the best, fastest, easiest, most trusted platform for both buyers and sellers to use. Each year, it could develop its platform in any number of different ways but where would it get the greatest return on investment?

Eamonn Galvin: In the digital world, the biggest lever you have is your product investment. You're always looking to drive value through their interaction with the site. In the online digital world, NPS is very powerful at helping to develop the product road map. Typically, the challenge in online businesses is they just have so many technical offerings that they can build out and in the absence of good customer data, the decisions on what to actually implement – well, the effort in many cases can be wasted. This is much more the case than in the offline world, because in the online world you can pretty much build software and solutions to solve any problem. You actually have an unlimited set of potential options to choose from but you're incurring significant expense for any of those options, so being able to apply a customer-centric metric becomes extremely important in terms of driving the development and the return on investment.

eBay had no shortage of data to help inform these investment decisions – from transactional details to customer net promoter score data. It used that data very effectively, but Amazon always seemed to be one step ahead in terms of customer intimacy and customer advocacy.

Eamonn Galvin: It's interesting when you look back to 2008, 2009, 2010, eBay's market position would have been very, very close relative to Amazon in the UK. We had NPS data as we were doing our own NPS surveys and we were also tracking Amazon's scores and Amazon was always ahead of eBay on NPS. If you fast forward, the growth trajectories of the two companies have been very different. Now there's many reasons for Amazon's incredible growth but they consistently had very high and very strong NPS scores.

Those trajectories are worth comparing. When Galvin joined eBay at the start of 2008, its share price was $13. Ten years later, it had risen to $40 – just short of a four-fold increase. Over the same period, Amazon's share price rose from $89 to $1229 – a fourteen-fold increase. Today, Amazon has a market value of nearly $900 billion compared to $35 billion for eBay. In very simplistic terms, Amazon managed to develop its product offering and satisfy its customers more effectively than eBay. The proof that the product was superior was there to be seen in both the Net Promoter Score feedback and in the company's growth. Throughout that decade, Amazon stayed closer to its customers and delivered greater shareholder value than eBay could manage.

In summary, less is more. A focused product range, designed and developed in conjunction with the customer will always work better than a large unwieldy incoherent collection of offerings. Be very clear about what that focused product range is and consistently update and investing in it, based purely on what customers need rather than what the product management team or the CEO thinks.

The Organisational Component

The third key component of strategy is not a traditional organisational strategy but more around ensuring that the company is organised to best meet the needs of its customers. For starters, if you agree with the earlier points around the Customer Component, the company's account management structure must align with its customer segmentation. Companies should not have multiple sales people knocking on the doors of the same client. Ideally there should be one account manager with overall responsibility for each client. Second, if you agree with the points about the Product Component, the product teams need to be much closer to the customer than they are in many organisations. Third, at a leadership level, does the company need a Chief Customer Officer or equivalent? Remember the Jeff Bezos story about the 'empty chair'? Who at the highest level of the organisation will represent the voice of the customer at senior executive meetings?

One of the first things that Colm O'Neill did when he came across to the UK with BT was to implement a single point of contact (SPOC) strategy for his account teams. At its heart, BT is a product company and one of the consequences of that strong product heritage was a situation where some corporate accounts had three or four different product managers selling into the same client, but there was no person with sole responsibility for understanding the entirety of that client's needs and translating those needs into an overall strategic solution.

Colm O'Neill: We're working hard at the moment to build clear accountability in BT. In a big complex organisation like BT, it can be quite easy to disperse accountability, and blame for things. It can be quite easy to intellectualise the problems that you're seeing and what's going on, and not own them yourself. In all of these situations, someone's got to own and be accountable for it. We were very clear the account manager owned it.

This single point of contact (SPOC) philosophy fits into the customer segmentation discussion as well, as most companies will strive to put their best account managers onto the largest or most strategically important accounts. Excellent account managers become trusted advisors to their clients so it is important for sales directors and senior executive teams to make the right decisions about who to assign to which clients, and how to build career paths that reward excellence in account management.

Colm O'Neill: The role of the account manager in customer experience is enormous because they take you from being a supplier organisation, to being a partner. If you provide good service delivery, then you're a good supplier and the customer experience score reflects that they are broadly happy with you. They'll probably be neutral, and they might even recommend you at a stretch. If you have a great account manager, supported by great service in the back end, that takes you to becoming a true business partner, and they say 'Actually, we can now not do without this organisation' because they don't just engage with you when they have a requirement, they engage with you when they're thinking about their strategy. It's that ability of the account manager to gain the trust and have the understanding of the customer environment where they know what will make a difference and what won't make a difference. It's also important to have the understanding of their own company environment that they're able to pull people together to answer all the questions a client will have.

A final point about the organisational dimension to a company's customer strategy is that of recruitment. One of the things that came out strongly in our interviews with Colm O'Neill and Gavin Patterson at BT was the important of having a very clear policy for recruiting and promoting people who really do believe in putting the customer at the heart.

Chapter 10 – Why Strategy is Important

Strategic planning is an inherent responsibility of the leadership team. If you now believe that customer centricity needs to be an essential component of your organisation's strategic plan, this Part is where we give you some guidance on developing that strategy.

How do 'Strategy' and 'Tactics' Relate?

There have been many disagreements about the blurred line between strategy and tactics, so it's important that we declare our view so that the purpose of each of these two parts is clear.

Benjamin B. Tregoe and John W. Zimmerman (in their book 'Top Management Strategy') draw the distinction as follows:

> Benjamin B. Tregoe and John W. Zimmerman: To understand what strategy is and how it relates to the operating side of the business, consider two facets which are critical to the survival of organisations: what the organisation wants to be and how it should get there. While both these facets are integral to long-range thinking, they must not be confused.... Since what the organisation wants to be sets the direction, it must be formulated prior to long-range planning and the day-to-day decision making that follows from such planning. We define strategy as the framework which guides those choices that determine the nature and direction of the organisation. Those choices relate to the scope of an organisation's products and services, markets, key capabilities, growth, return, and allocation of resources.

Therefore, we perceive 'strategy' to be the long-term view (the purpose of the organisation) that the leadership team has determined and is usually articulated in a succinct 'Mission Statement'. One part of that statement might read: "To be Earth's most customer-centric company, where customers can find and discover anything they might want to buy online, and endeavours to offer its customers the lowest possible prices." (Amazon)

'Tactics' are therefore focused upon the short-term and are much more about actions that will contribute to achievement of the Mission. Tactics are the detailed steps that are usually incorporated into a plan. "The art of disposing armed forces in order of battle and of organising operations, especially during contact with an enemy." (Oxford Dictionary).

In this book we address the specific tactics of implementing a customer centricity project in Part IV Tactics & Execution.

While we are discussing terminology – it is very likely that the many initiatives that emerge in an organisation might be called projects or programmes (or programs). The generally accepted definition (at least in the profession of project management) is that a program(me) consists a group of projects. We have opted here to use the term 'programme' to describe the design and implementation of customer centricity in an organisation. The Customer Centricity Programme is likely to spawn a number of individual survey, remedial and improvement projects that might well be managed as a wider programme by the organisation.

Figure 8 shows the structural relationship between projects programmes and portfolios. The process is as follows:

- Strategy is determined whilst being cognisant of the environment (Strategy)
- A Vison for the desired future state of the organisation is articulated (Leadership)

- A Portfolio Management layer is authorised to control the many change projects that will emerge
- Change Projects are identified (several spawned by customer centricity initiatives)
- Some projects are a natural cluster and are managed as a Programme
- Each Change Project is executed and produces changes to the Operations and Service delivery of the organisation (Tactics & Execution)
- Those changes deliver benefits to the organisation, ultimately contributing to the achievement of the Vision and influencing future Strategy (Culture & Change)

Figure 8 – CX Programme – Conceptual Model

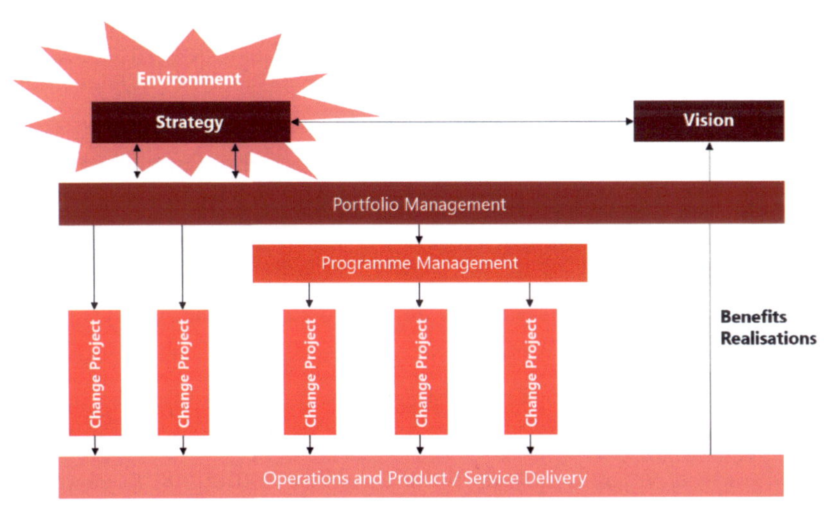

Are We Selling Products or Servicing Customers?

The traditional business approach is to design and build a product (or service) and the customers will come rushing to your door. We know that's not true anymore, however many companies are stuck in the past because it's always been a safe place to operate. Major decisions at the leadership level are often based upon the current product/service offering with, of course, the customer in mind – but we assume we will always know what the customer will want.

This view, in the real world, is changing. We know that disruption is occurring in many industries and competition is now global. The traditional barriers to entry that have protected businesses are disappearing.

The new approach is to link product and service strategies to customers' needs and that's not by assuming that you know what the customer wants – it's through asking the customer what they perceive they need and researching what solutions will best meet those needs.

Christine Corbett: We needed to look at ourselves and ask, "what is it now that our customers want us to do?" Customers just want you to get the basics right first. Then they'll give you the permission to enter into new interesting opportunities.

The other perspective that is worth contemplating in your strategy setting sessions is the nature of your company's interactions with customers. Even within B2B relationships there are likely to be both 'transactional' and 'relationship' interactions. Transactional is when purchasing is virtually automatic and, unless something goes wrong, the transactions will continue uninterrupted into the future.

The more complex (and usually costly) purchasing can be described as 'relationship' interactions. These are commonly the province of the account manager or sales teams and often involve face-to-face meetings. Remember that in both types of interactions, customer loyalty should feature in your strategic planning for reasons of retaining customers.

We'll discuss later the importance of taking 'relationship management' to a new level as part of a customer centricity project, but it's important to consider that for significant customers (strategic accounts) in a B2B environment, the customer experience must engage all levels of the supplier organisation. The CEO should expect to have a relationship with the customer's CEO, the account management team should include operations, support, finance members (even if they don't have personal contact with customers) and the relationship focus must extend all the way down to the physical delivery of the products and services.

Competitive Positioning

Most companies will experience new market entrants with new products and services that will compete with them for market share. To survive in this environment, you have to be extraordinarily focused on what you are good at, and how you can add value.

Colm O'Neill: Inefficiency in the business shows up in dissatisfied customers. If your customers are satisfied, your processes and systems are probably efficient and they are prepared to pay more money for a better service. We've always tracked the financial dividend that we get from happy customers. At renewal time, happy customers are less aggressive in a negotiation. They keep value in the deal. It's a self-fulfilling prophecy. It was a customer service philosophy that stayed at the company for years and years. EMC became the top performing stock on the New York Stock Exchange for the years 1990 to 2000. It went through phenomenal growth.

Many industries are experiencing disruption and this is unlikely to change as technology continues to advance. Disruption means new competitors taking market share and customers willing to switch to a competitor because there are often few barriers to changing suppliers. The one differentiator that secures customer loyalty is customer centricity and this means increased focus on relationship management and account planning.

B2B2C and B2B2B

As explained earlier, B2B2C usually describes a customer environment where the supplier is selling through an intermediary channel such as a broker or reseller. A key concept for an executive team embarking upon a customer-centricity journey is to understand what your customer's customer is thinking. This is often referred to as B2B2C (business to business to consumer) but can also apply where the customer's customer is another business (B2B2B).

The reason why it is important to be able to 'see through' your client to understand who their customers are and their needs, is to gain a deeper appreciation of the issues your customer is facing in their business. This appreciation then enables tailoring of your products and services to help your customer to be even more successful with their customers. In a competitive environment this is a powerful differentiator that enhances loyalty.

An example we encountered was that of DuluxGroup which is an Australian company whose origins date back to 1918 when the business was established in Sydney as a paint manufacturer. Today it sells a wide range of decorator and building products under a variety of brand names including B&D, Cabot's, Dulux, Parchem, Selleys and Yates. These brands are sold through household hardware chains such as Bunnings. For many years the company had identified their primary customers as retailers such as large hardware store chains and a major part of their focus was on bidding for shelf space in these stores against competitors. More recently they realised that the retailers are just an intermediary (albeit an important one) and that their real customers are the consumers, home decorators and professional painters. They have now geared their brand marketing and their relationship-building to reach both their B2B2B and their B2B2C customers.

Trust

In the end, relationships are about trust. Trust between individuals and between organisations.

We have taken the opportunity to include a useful explanation of trust in a business environment. This definition of the levels of trust is derived from 'The Trust Ladder', by Mark Hollyoake & Peter Lavers

Level 1. Co-existence

Co-existence refers to a state where the suppliers and customers occupy the same market/sector space. The relationship exists on a transactional level with little knowledge or understanding of each other. The focus is often product driven or led, with a supplier's product meeting a basic need or specification.

Level 2. Shallow Dependence

This is underpinned through these drivers of trustworthiness at this level:

- Discretion
- Reliability
- Competence

This is enabled through Risk - or Calculus - based trust.

Level 3. Shallow Interdependence

This is where most vendors and customers start to develop mutual value through a more structured relationship, having established a trading relationship through the Shallow Dependence stage. It is underpinned through these drivers of trustworthiness at this level:

- Predictability
- Consistency

It is enabled through Knowledge or Competence - based trust.

Level 4. Deep Dependence

This is where most vendors wish they had given more thought to relational development and its implications. At this stage the vendor has developed relationships with a core group of customers and they have become dependent upon the customers for their value and volume delivery. The balance and onus of trust and equitability is dependent upon the customers. A Deeply Dependent relationship is underpinned by:

- Integrity
- Concern
- Benevolence

A key relational driver of this level of relationship is the network of relationships and how they are managed.

Level 5. Deep Interdependence

"We need and rely on each other for our success within the market." Deep Interdependence is the ultimate aim of B2B customer management and the culmination of well executed B2B relationship development. At this stage, the vendor has developed strategic relationships with a core group of customers in which they have become interdependent on each other for their value, volume potential and delivery. The balance and onus of trust and equitability is dependent on the other in a way that is acceptable to both parties. Identification based trust also underpins a Deeply Interdependent relationship and supports:

- Foresight
- Intuition
- Empathy

Relationship drivers: shared meaning, values, products, goals

Indicators of High Levels of Trust

- Joint working processes
- Shared vision and strategy (to create value)
- Early adoption of innovative ideas
- High levels of loyalty
- Customer as an ambassador
- Increased share of business
- Potential for co-location

Mick McCarthy is a 30-year banking veteran and heads up Santander's business and corporate banking division in Poland. For Mick, trust is a key - if not the key - component of a business banking relationship.

Mick McCarthy: All of the research proves that the more you invest in a relationship and the more customer feels that you understand their business, then there is a correlation between that and loyalty, and between that and the level of business that you do with customers.

When Eamonn Galvin was at eBay, one of the key insights he had was that revenues and profitability were driven by the average purchase price of items on the eBay marketplace. The challenge was to drive up that average purchase price. The net promoter score data showed that the key to success was to improve buyers' trust in the platform and that formed the thinking behind the 'Buyer Protection Programme' which guaranteed that buyers received a 30-day guarantee on any product bought on eBay.

Eamonn Galvin: What NPS uncovered was the importance of trust as a key driver of NPS and what trust does is allows customers to purchase higher value items. Over time NPS enabled us to correlate trust with its impact on revenue. We ran a trust programme, the Buyer Protection Program, which took on all of the responsibility of making good for buyers in the event that they had a negative incident on eBay.

Gaining Commitment

We know that customer centricity has to start at the top. It has to be believed in and committed to by the senior executive team. But we see many of these of initiatives where they're then driven downwards, and those staff on the receiving end say: ‘here comes the next flavour of the month”. To work effectively, the commitment process in an organisation has to be collaborative. This involves not only the leaders demonstrating commitment, but communicating what, why and how we are going to become more customer centric.

A related challenge that is more prevalent in a large and dispersed organisation is the probability of a disconnect between what senior leadership is thinking and what is actually happening at the customer interface. Strategies developed by management can easily become diluted as they trickle down through the organisation. Customer centricity strategies that are not communicated clearly and that are seen to be the latest 'management trend' can be resisted and ignored. We have more to say on this topic in Part V - Culture & Change.

Corporate Values

Many organisations enthusiastically state their customer focus in their statement of corporate values. An example is the Peoplebank Promise. Peoplebank is Australia's largest IT recruitment and contracting company with more than 4500 contractors and 600 permanent placements each year. Their promise:

- As a proud member of the Peoplebank team, I believe that extraordinary customer service is not a collection of words but a set of consistent actions and behaviours.
- Everything I do is passionately directed at delighting you, our customer, by always delivering on my promises.
- I want Peoplebank to be your number one choice in recruitment. I know that your trust and loyalty can only be earned by being accountable to deliver on the promises I make.

Australia Post's Christine Corbett had a similar approach to being clear about what the company's values were, when it came to customers. She called them Customer Priorities.

Christine Corbett: It doesn't matter what gets said around a boardroom table, it's the people on the front line who are critical in any customer experience, so if they believe it, the customers will see it.

We came up with four customer priorities:

- Delivering seamless customer experiences
- Listening to customers and taking action
- Knowing our customers
- Empowering our people

Project Management Methodology

One of the mistakes we have seen is where organisations embark upon a customer centricity project without a structured approach to planning and executing a formal project. The adverse consequences can include:

- Lack of a valid Business Case justifying the project
- Unrealistic expectations that are never met
- Objectives not properly defined and agreed
- Poor estimation of duration and costs
- Inadequate definition and acceptance of roles
- Lack of risk management
- Inadequate planning and co-ordination of resources
- Lack of communication and stakeholder management

Many of these mistakes can be eliminated by having a clear business case and project plan.

As an example of a more rigorous approach to project management within this book we will utilise some components of the PRINCE2 project management methodology. PRINCE2 has its origins with the UK Government as early as 1989 and is administrated by Axelos Ltd. It has been adopted widely across the world as a structured and reliable approach to project management. The advantages of PRINCE2 include its flexibility to be adapted to any type of project and its ability to be scaled up or down to suit the size of any project.

PRINCE2 has 7 processes:

- Starting Up a project, when a business case and project brief are developed and the project team is appointed
- Initiating a project, when the project documentation (including project plan and communications plan) is created and approved
- Directing a project, which recommends the ways in which management oversees the project
- Controlling a Stage, suggests how each stage should be controlled
- Managing Product Delivery, manages the creation of the deliverables of the project
- Managing Stage Boundaries, guides the transition from one stage to the next
- Closing a project, covers the closure, follow-on actions and evaluation of the benefits

In this Part (Strategy) we will only address the Business Case within the process of Starting Up a Customer Centricity Project, because it is 'strategic' in nature. The ensuing processes will be covered in Part IV (Tactics & Execution). We will use a minimalist version of PRINCE2 to keep our project management approach reasonably simple and manageable to be applied by teams who may not be familiar with PRINCE2.

Chapter 11 - Business Case

Writing the Business Case

A customer centricity project is likely to have had its origins in a leadership review of business performance. As demonstrated in the case study examples in Part II – Leadership, there are many possible triggers to embarking down the path of customer centricity. Those triggers might include recent performance shortfalls, loss of market share, disruption or major changes in strategy.

A well-defined and robust business case is essential to a customer centricity project for several reasons:

- It provides a clear justification for the monetary costs and the resource commitment
- It defines the benefits expected to be derived from the project and provides an opportunity to measure those benefits as they are realised
- It enables the leadership team to decide if the initiative is desirable, viable and achievable
- It informs those involved in delivering the project of the high-level expectations of the organisation
- Without a business case there is a risk of lack of commitment by all involved and a consequent probability of failure

The business case is the document that answers the question: "Why should this project be done?" It is therefore critical to the success of a customer centricity project. If the business case cannot present a persuasive argument for proceeding (usually based upon financial outcomes) then it is highly likely to be rejected by the leadership team.

Like all investment decisions, the leadership team should first evaluate how well a customer centricity project aligns with the organisation's strategic plans and how well it will contribute to the corporate objectives.

The business case is focused upon 'benefits', which are, by definition, 'the measurable improvements resulting from an outcome that is perceived as an advantage by one or more stakeholders'.

The development of the business case should be undertaken by an individual or a small group assigned by the leadership team. They will need to work closely with the leadership team members to ensure that congruence and commitment are achieved – because ultimately it is the leadership team (including the senior leader) who must take ownership of the business case. It is the leadership team who will approve the business case and allow the project to commence.

The initial business case should be prepared very early in the lifecycle of the project because the leadership team will be unwilling to invest in the planning process, and certainly won't allow execution to commence, unless they are confident that it is desirable, viable and achievable.

Christine Corbett: Although we had an overarching customer focus blueprint, each initiative had to have an individual business case underneath it, because we needed to achieve community and commercial objectives which involved testing and learning and proving out the concepts. We showed both customer and financial impacts (in terms of revenue growth or efficiency) of those decisions and we were able to demonstrate to our sales teams that when you improve NPS

(Net Promoter Score), the number of repeat purchases and parcel volumes increases.

The challenge for those charged with developing the business case is that, at this early stage, very little estimating and scheduling will have been undertaken and therefore the initial projections of costs, resources and timescale are unlikely to be precise. This will be easier if a previous customer centricity project had been completed by the organisation, or, it may be practical to derive estimates from information from similar organisations who have undertaken a customer centricity project.

The business case therefore needs to be well founded and defendable. Its primary purpose is the justification of the project based upon the expected benefits. It can be challenging to quantify the benefits in what is essentially an organisational culture change process. The business case will require some persuasive arguments to convince the decision-makers that there is sufficient evidence that customer centricity will cause a significant improvement on the bottom line in a reasonable time-frame.

Our advice, when embarking upon writing a business case, is to talk to others who have done this sort of transformation before, and to professionals who work in this sphere. Their experiences need to be translated for your environment but will usually provide an informed basis for a sound business case. Of course, there is always the do-nothing argument to be considered with the question "what are the consequences if the organisation does not transition to become more customer-centric?". Think about it!

Be wary of those who suggest that the project could be done on a 'shoe-string' using existing resources and existing in-house skills. A half-baked implementation that fails is likely to set the organisation back even further than its starting position and inhibit future transformation projects.

It is highly likely that the project will be broken into stages such as:

- Customer survey stage
- Urgent initiatives stage
- Culture change stage
- Long-term initiatives stage (or individual projects)

Projections (costs, resources and timescale) for each of these stages will need to be developed, although both the urgent initiatives and long-term initiatives are unlikely to be known at this time. If they emerge as major initiatives (e.g. replacement of core systems) they will need to be isolated as separate projects, each with their own business case.

The initial business case should become a 'living' document that is updated and adjusted as the planning process proceeds. It is also likely that the business case will need to be adjusted (with approval) as the project is executed. Risks, issues and proposed changes to the project do occur and could impact the costs, resources, timescale and the benefits expected. Note that if, at any time, the project is no longer desirable, viable and achievable then it should be stopped.

Another aspect to be aware of, is that the realisation of the benefits is unlikely to be immediate. Most often the initiatives and the change in culture are likely to take time to have an impact. It is not unusual for financial gains to become visible some six or 12 months after the project is commenced and it may take years to fully realise the total range of benefits expected. We recommend that Benefits Reviews of a customer centricity project should be included in the agenda of all leadership team meetings.

A danger associated with this slow realisation of the benefits emerges when the customer centricity project becomes focused entirely on delivering a customer survey and the identified initiatives without measuring outcomes and consequent benefits.

Gavin Patterson: You have to put a business case around it. There are no free rides. The calls on capital, calls on OPEX within the business are multiple. I wouldn't expect any project team to feel as though they just have the right to spend money on a wing and a prayer, and even within the multitude of things you can do to improve your customer satisfaction, you have to be able to prioritise.

We recall what David Thodey said earlier. Telstra based its business case on reduction of churn (loss of customers) and the lifetime value of the customer including the propensity of the customers to buy multiple products. They realised that they had to include a $60m budget to put in place a system that would measure interactions, product satisfaction, process satisfaction, and make the data available in real time.

Rewards & Recognition Strategy

One component of cost to be included in the Business Case should be that of the rewards to be made available to employees.

Many organisations recognise that rewards and recognition for employees are vital to encourage on-going participation and improved results. There are three types of rewards that can each have either (or both) a monetary element and recognition in front of peers.

They are:

- Rewards and recognition for actively engaging in the effective recruiting of customers to participate in the survey stage. The success of the survey is geared to the participation rate.
- Rewards and recognition for gaining very positive survey results, either individually or by groups. Peer comparisons can, of course, be both positive and negative.
- Rewards and recognition for attaining the customer centricity project objectives such as increased revenue, profitability, customer retention etc.

Note that these are logically linked to the KPIs and targets that should have been identified in developing the Business Case.

The structure of a rewards and recognition strategy needs to be considered – what are the objectives, who is rewarded on which results, how do we measure success, how and when are the rewards and recognition delivered.

There are many other forms of rewards ranging from personal vouchers or gift cards to commercially provided employee incentive programmes.

Mairead McSweeney: We talked about rewarding people who do well. Some of the verbatim comments from our customers talked about our people being our biggest asset. Let's recognise that, and let's embed it and plan a big celebration to highlight what our customers have said. Lots of work done, more to do, but reward people, make it part of their day job. We put 'Customer First' into 10% of their Pay Plan so that people were rewarded. For every single person that was named we created an email that would say: a customer went out of their way to name you in their verbatim comments, we just want to thank you for all the good work. There might be a 25 or 50 quid voucher in it. But in some cases, where it was just the name in the comments, every single one of them got an email from the MD thanking them and copying in their manager and their sales director.

Telstra's David Thodey had a similar approach to target setting and payment of bonuses.

David Thodey: We were all on one target, and everybody had their own target. Right down to a call centre, to a shop, to the product manager. It started off with the accountants and other guys saying “well, I never talk to customers, why are you paying me on this, I'm in the background”, and we said; “now hang on, how about your family, your friends, people you know”. And slowly everyone sort-of bought in.

Contents of a Business Case

- Executive summary
- Reasons for the project
- Options considered
- Expected benefits
- Expected dis-benefits
- Rewards and Recognition Strategy
- Timescale
- Costs
- Investment appraisal
- Major risks

Executive summary

Provide a quick overview of 'what' the project is about and 'why' it exists (the benefits expected).

Reasons for the project

Explain how well the customer centricity project will enable the achievement of the corporate strategies and objectives.

Options considered

Options that were considered and a realistic assessment of the desirability (attractiveness), viability (practicability) and achievability (potential for success) of each of these options:

- Do nothing
- Do the bare minimum
- Do the project properly

State the recommended option.

Expected benefits

List the benefits (both financial and non-financial) and record against each benefit:

- Current status
- How the benefit can be measured?
- Expected measurable improvement
- Who is responsible for this benefit?

Benefits should be assessed by the leadership team to determine if they are realistic or over-optimistic.

You might also argue that you can acquire more customers. If, for example, you provide a faster way of providing the customer's expected service, or you might be able to remove a real negative versus a competitor.

Expected dis-benefits

A dis-benefit is a negative outcome that could result from executing this project. The leadership team will need to have visibility of these consequences and will judge if the benefits exceed the dis-benefits.

Rewards & Recognition Strategy

State your intended KPIs and targets for the project and ensure that the cost of rewards is included in the costs.

Timescale

- Proposed start date
- Proposed completion date
- When will costs be incurred?
- When will resources be consumed?
- When will benefits accrue?

Costs

- Costs expected for each stage
- Resources required for each stage
- Ongoing support costs
- Future possible costs

Investment appraisal

Apply whatever investment appraisal methods are used in the organisation – Return on Investment, Payback Period, Discounted Cash Flow, Net Present Value etc.

Major risks

Identify any major risks that could adversely affect the project. These might include the impact of any other projects that are likely to run concurrently.

Return on Investment (ROI)

In 2019 Pointillist published a paper titled 'Calculating the ROI of Customer Experience'. Although they mostly focused on B2C businesses, there are some useful suggestions.

They stress the need for a quantitative assessment of ROI to make a strong business case, rather than simply stating the 'soft' benefits.

The suggested business metrics for the 'Return' component are:

Revenue

They refer to a recent Forrester study that found that revenue of CX leaders outgrew the revenue of CX laggard competitors by 5 to 1.

Forrester calculate a Customer Experience Index which is based upon CX quality (effectiveness, ease, emotion) and customer loyalty (advocacy, enrichment, retention). Across 13 different consumer categories they estimated that a 1% increase in the index resulted in an average increase in spend of about $17 per consumer. When multiplied by the number of customers, this is a substantial increase in revenue for each company. The numbers for a B2B company might be different but are likely to be quite positive.

Customer Retention

Forrester states that customers who have a high-quality experience are 2.7 times more likely to keep doing business with a brand than customers who have a low-quality experience.

Cross Sell and Upsell

Satisfied customers are more open to proposals from their preferred supplier to purchase additional products or services, or to upgrade their purchase.

Reduced Cost-to-Serve

This is clearly a significant cost in B2C transactions where customer care centres are involved and may not be as important a measure in B2B relationships. Perhaps B2B customer contact should be viewed more as an opportunity for account managers to interact with customers and enhance relationships.

The suggested business metrics for the 'Investment' component:

Training

The paper recommends costing an investment in training employees on products and services and cross training with the roles of other teams to better respond to customers.

We would add that training in customer centricity is a worthwhile investment.

Technology

Consider the need to upgrade CRM systems, analytics applications and possibly self-service channel integration.

Operating Costs

Investments can include new customer and employee apps, websites and it is here that the costs of customer surveys needs to be estimated. There is also consideration to be given to the staffing and support costs of the culture change towards customer centricity.

The ROI Calculation

Accumulating the 'Returns' (benefits) in the form of increased profits derived from improved customer centricity and comparing it to the direct cost of the 'Investment' enables the ROI formula to be applied:

ROI% = 100*(Benefits – Investments)/Investments

Example Business Case – Customer Centricity Project

Executive summary

This project will identify opportunities for the company to become more customer-centric based upon a survey of existing customers. It will provide an action plan of initiatives that will reduce customer churn and increase revenue to deliver an increase in net profit of 6% from an investment of $200,000.

Reasons for the project

1. The corporate strategy for next year forecasts a growth in sales revenue of 5% and an increase in net profit of 10%. These cannot be achieved fully through new products and services. A focus on customer centricity has been identified as a strategic goal over the next two years.

Specific objectives for next year include the following:

- Customer churn reduced from 10% p.a. to 5% p.a.
- Increase in revenue from existing customers of 8%.

2. Aggregate corporate Net Promoter Score has fallen from +5 to -10 in 12 months.

Options considered

Option	Desirability	Viability	Achievability
Do nothing	Attractive because it does not divert sales resources	Very easy	Will not enable corporate objectives to be achieved
Do the bare minimum	Unattractive because it is unlikely to have a major impact on	Requires some effort and some changes	Still requires some cost and use of internal resources but corporate

	reducing customer churn		objectives will not be achieved
Do the project properly	Attractive because it will focus the entire organisation on customers	Will be viable if funding allocated and resource diversion approved	Expected to enable achievement of corporate objectives

The recommended option is to implement a customer centricity project properly.

Expected benefits

Benefit	**Current status**	**Expected measurable improvement**	**How the benefit can be measured**	**Who is responsible for this benefit**
Increased net profit	Current year expected to be 6% of revenue	Increase to 7% of revenue	Accounting reports	Sales, Operations
Improved employee morale	Recent climate survey indicates total employee job satisfaction at 70%	Increase to 80%	Annual climate survey	Team leaders

Expected dis-benefits

Diversion of sales resources to improving existing customer relationships may adversely affect acquisition of new customers.

Rewards & Recognition Strategy

KPIs and targets for this coming year will be established as follows:

- % customers who respond to the customer survey – 50%
- NPS scores – achievement of +10
- Increase in revenue from existing customers – 8%

Achievement of these targets will contribute to a pay bonus (at the end of the year) of up to 10% of base pay. 5% will be calculated on individual team results and 5% on overall company results.

Timescale

- Proposed start date – January next year
- Proposed completion date – December next year
- When will costs be incurred? – Customer survey in January/February
- When will resources be consumed? – January to April
- When will benefits accrue? – expect to see initial results in July, increasing further by December

Costs

Stage	Timing	Costs expected for each stage	Resources required for each stage	Ongoing support costs	Future possible costs
Customer survey	January/February	$50,000 external survey firm	Nil	Nil	Likely to repeat customer survey in following year
CX Programme Team	January to June	$50,000 (already sunk cost)	1 FTE plus 10% of sales team time for 4 months	In-house resources	Likely repeat next year
Urgent initiatives	April to June	Estimate $100,000	IT department staff for 3 months	Finance to provide new reports	Nil

Culture change	March to December	$50,000 rewards costs	People and Culture staff to implement	Rewards systems	Re-design of remuneration plans
Long-term initiatives	July and beyond	Not identified at this time	Not identified at this time	Not identified at this time	Not identified at this time

Investment appraisal

Total investment $200,000, internal resource costs absorbed, increase in net profit $50,000 in first year, $150,000 in second year – payback period two years.

Major risks

- Lack of commitment to the project by sales teams.
- Possible impact from restructuring in one region.

Summary of Part III

- Define Customer, Product and Organisation components
- Strategy is about Why? Tactics are about How?
- Focus has shifted from product/service first to customer first
- Customer centricity is a competitive differentiator
- Trust is at the core a customer centricity strategy
- Commitment from the CEO and the leadership team is vital
- Implement a customer centricity strategy as a project
- Write the Business Case that justifies the investment in customer centricity

Part IV – Tactics & Execution

Chapter 12 - Starting up the Customer Centricity Project

- The Transition from Strategy to Tactics
- Pilot vs Big Bang
- Follow the Money
- Developing a Project Brief
- Anticipate Governance
- Results Reporting Plan
- Achieving Robust B2B Survey Participation Rates
- KPIs and Targets
- Example Project Brief

Chapter 13 – Tactical Planning

- Chief Customer Officer (CCO)
- Selecting a Project Team
- Responsibilities of the Project Team
- Restructures
- Initiating the Project
- Risk Analysis
- Quality and Governance
- Systems, Reporting, Data Security and Crisis Management
- Communications Plan
- Project Planning & Resourcing

Chapter 14 - Executing the Plan

- Controlling a Stage
- Progress Review Meetings

- Assessing the Customer Survey Results
- Capturing, Defining, Prioritising and Allocating Action Items
- Closing the Loop with Customers

Chapter 15 - Completing the Project

- Project Closure
- Follow-on Actions & Joint Action Plans
- Evaluating Benefits

Chapter 16 - Account Management

Summary of Part IV

"Strategy without tactics is the slowest route to victory. Tactics without strategy is the noise before defeat."

- Sun Tzu

"Execution is a specific set of behaviors and techniques that companies need to master in order to have competitive advantage. It's a discipline of its own."

- Ram Charan and Larry Bossidy, Execution

"The result of bad communication is a disconnection between strategy and execution."

- Chuck Martin, former vice president, IBM

Chapter 12 - Starting up the Customer Centricity Project

The Transition from Strategy to Tactics

As we have suggested, responsibility for defining the strategy rests with the leadership group. However, as the finite details of the Project Brief, Selection of the Project Team and Business Case are refined, it is likely that the project team will have become intimately involved.

At this point momentum and enthusiasm will be building to commence the project and the customer centricity journey. Therefore, it is important that the leadership team become re-engaged at this time to make the critical decision as to whether the project is desirable, viable and achievable, based upon what has been presented thus far. They must be confident that the benefits indicated can be realised, or it's back to the proverbial drawing board.

If the decision is 'GO' then the project team is formally activated and takes responsibility for delivery. This does not mean that the leadership team relinquishes its role – their ongoing commitment and participation are vital for a successful outcome.

In their book 'Execution – The Discipline of Getting Things Done' Larry Bossidy and Ram Charan converse on three building blocks of execution:

A. The leader's seven essential behaviours:

1. Know your people and your business
2. Insist on realism
3. Set clear goals and priorities

4. Follow through
5. Reward the doers
6. Expand people's capabilities
7. Know thyself

B. Creating the framework for cultural change

C. Having the right people in the right place

Once the strategic decision to become more customer centric has been agreed the business case is developed to justify the costs (Writing a Business Case is described in Part III – Strategy). Included in these, as well as any direct expenditure, should be the human resource costs. A customer centricity programme is unlikely to succeed unless it has some dedicated people assigned to the project – even if their roles are part-time. We will define their roles in this Part.

The reasons behind a customer centricity project and the objectives need to be clearly articulated to all staff by the leaders, otherwise the organisation's commitment to the programme can be questioned. If the programme is judged to be 'just another fad that will pass' the integrity of the data collection and the interpretation of the findings will fail to achieve the desired outcomes.

Also, account managers may perceive that a customer survey as an intrusion into their relationships with their customers and negative views of the survey may be communicated to customers. This is unlikely to occur if they understand the reasons for the programme and see that senior management is committed to enhancing customer relationships over the long term.

Make it clear that the survey is a diagnostic and analytical tool which provides actionable data about problems identified and that there will be an issue-resolution opportunity after the survey.

Pilot vs Big Bang

There is likely to be a vigorous discussion about the merits of a 'pilot project' versus a full implementation across the organisation. The advantages of a pilot (or trial) are that resource commitment is likely to be lower and that the validity of the business case (the benefits realised) can be assessed before a wider implementation. The disadvantages are that a full implementation (and its benefits) are delayed and it is possible that cross-organisational changes to improve customer centricity will be inhibited. Interestingly, most of the projects that we have seen started off as pilots, even if they weren't called pilots at the time. This is likely to be a scale decision - small companies probably don't need to pilot but most really large organisations seem to do so.

Follow the Money

This is one of John O'Connor's favourite statements. The principle behind it is important – the whole purpose of a customer centricity project is to deliver better bottom line results and to position the company for a secure future. Therefore, the project strategy needs to focus on the customers that are of most value to the organisation now and into the future. This is leverage on the bottom line.

Some customer survey approaches are to take a selected sample across the entire spectrum of customers, others, even more ambitious, are to attempt a census of all customers. Neither approach will deliver the short-term insights that will emerge from 'follow the money'.

Developing a Project Brief

The starting point for the Project Brief is to describe the project in writing so that the various key decision makers within the leadership team, can understand and interpret what is proposed. The Project Brief is a short document that describes the Customer Centricity Project. It is usually prepared by the proposer of the customer centricity project who might be the Sales Director in consultation with the CEO. It usually includes these topics:

- Background
- Objectives
- Scope
- Approach
- Stakeholder Engagement

Its companion documents is the Business Case (developed in the Strategy phase).

Background

The Project Brief is intended to communicate the essence of customer centricity project to the key stakeholders – these might include board members and the staff members who will contribute to the project.

Therefore, it is useful to provide a context so that the readers can understand why the project has emerged. It is likely to explain what triggered the project and perhaps what has occurred in the past that has suggested that customer centricity should be on the corporate agenda.

Objectives

Is critical that clear objectives for a customer centricity programme are identified, discussed and agreed to ensure that internal expectations will be met and to design the appropriate survey questions.

Like all objectives they should be SMART:

- **S**pecific,
- **M**easurable,
- **A**chievable,
- **R**ealistic, and
- **T**imely

The objectives should consider the many reasons for assessing the quality of your organisation's relationships with its customers. These might emerge by asking these questions:

- How well are our customers' expectations are being met?
- What do they perceive are our strengths and weaknesses?
- How committed they are to the relationship?
- Which customers are at risk of defecting to competitors?
- How do customers perceive us compared with our competitors?
- Which areas within our business are performing well and which are not?
- How effective is our account management?
- What operational systems or services are not meeting customers' expectations?

Scope

The scope of the programme needs to be agreed. Are we addressing customer centricity across the entire organisation or only applying this programme to certain businesses, subsidiaries, or divisions? Are we covering multiple countries, states or regions?

The scope of a customer survey project needs consideration of how deep and how wide the data collection should be. These are some scope dimensions to consider:

- All customers vs high value customers only (top 20, 100 etc)
- Strategic vs Non-Strategic customers
- Specific market segments
- Geography – do we want to assess all regions, all branches, all offices
- Diversity of contacts within the customers to be assessed – do we include C-level executives, internal decision-makers, back-office staff, front-of-house staff, purchasing managers etc
- Customers we have assessed before and/or new customers
- Pilot vs Big Bang

Assuming that you have decided that a 'baseline' or initial customer survey is a logical first step it will be important to understand what the existing processes for customer contact are – who talks to who in customer organisations at various levels and for various activities (sales, service, manufacturing, delivery, help-desk etc)

For large organisations like Atos in the UK & Ireland, a smaller scope focusing initially on the largest clients ('Follow the Money' approach) was deemed to the most appropriate way to start.

Sue de Wit: You must be really clear on the scope that you want to achieve and start with a small area first, and then grow. Don't try and take everything on at once, because it's not all going to work.

The next step is to carefully plan the survey contact strategy. It should not be just a simple request for feedback from customers. You will get minimal response and possibly misleading information. Later we will lay out a step by step approach to designing a comprehensive survey contact strategy.

Care needs to be taken with segmentation when undertaking a survey with customers. Customers might be considered of similar size (in terms of revenue to the supplier) and possibly be categorised into the same industry segment, but their needs may be very different.

In the case of BT, this meant an evolving customer segmentation approach and contact strategy as the CX programme developed under Kathryn Whitehouse's leadership. Having previously led a sales team in BT, Whitehouse was in a good position to challenge any account managers whose contact strategy and proposed customer lists didn't match up to her expectations.

Kathryn Whitehouse: The process we've developed starts with getting the contact strategy right. Engaging and recruiting all of the contacts within your customer's organisation where you'll get most value from the feedback.

Approach

Stating the intended approach is primarily a preview of the Project Plan (yet to be developed). It gives the reader an insight into how the customer centricity project will be delivered. Note that the estimated costs and timescale need to be updated in the Business Case.

Many organisations embarking upon the customer centricity journey look first towards conducting a relationship survey to baseline the quality of their current relationships with key clients. They may be already collecting transactional NPS data but recognise that this is only giving them a snapshot of the current perception by customers – it rarely gives them insights into 'why' they are receiving the current scores.

The approach also needs to recognise the linkages to any internal quality systems that may be providing information on the quality of services being delivered, often focused upon operational service delivery, but with obvious consequences for customers.

Examples include: Quality Management Systems (QMS), Total quality Management (TQM), Continuous Quality Improvement (CQI), Six Sigma, Right First Time (RFT), Delivery In Full On time (DIFOT).

Joe Edwards: What that means is not just putting the plans in place and monitoring every quarter as usual. We would, in our top accounts, have account reviews with the executive board. It was making sure that the CEO and the CXO were all over our accounts on a regular basis. On those top accounts, we're going to spend time with them. We're going to prioritise our time and make several calls a week where we get out there and start talking properly to this client base.

Identify what recent survey projects have been undertaken. It is not uncommon for various departments or regions to have undertaken a diverse range of customer survey projects. The problem with this is that results are difficult to correlate across organisational boundaries. It's also important to take prior survey activity into consideration when anticipating survey fatigue.

Mairead McSweeney: I spent a couple of weeks literally just understanding what is the 'As Is' programme and one thing I noticed at the time was that there was little communication around the customer surveys. There was no holistic end-to-end communications to say: this is what we're doing; this is how we're doing it.

Stakeholder Engagement

We'll talk further about communications however it is important at this early stage that internal stakeholders are made aware of an emerging strategic plan that encompasses customer centricity. Why, because you need to signal the strategy early in the planning process to identify any potential pockets of resistance, and, it is likely that the various stakeholders will have ideas and positive contributions to make. A stakeholder engagement session is often an excellent way to open this conversation.

Sue de Wit: Make sure that you begin stakeholder management in your own organisation. What people hear, and how they interpret it, and what they're going to do are often so different. Make sure that you've got the key people that you need to influence on board. It's not just a case of your CEO dictating it and then everything will fall into place.

At the end of this chapter is an example Project Brief.

Anticipate Governance

Part of the planning process is to consider how to assure the integrity of the customer survey. There are multiple ways that internal people could possibly subvert the collection of meaningful data.

It's called 'gaming' and one obvious way is manipulation of the selection of customers to be surveyed. If an account manager or region manager, for example, wants to ensure a positive report then they will bias the selection of customers towards well-served and close-relationship customers. Setting clear rules and careful and independent monitoring of the customer selection process will overcome this tactic.

Shane O'Neill: There's a classic trick in transport operations when people measure transport metrics. It is to allow a lot of operational exceptions, which makes sense to an operator, but to a customer - they don't really care. Therefore, we planned to change that approach and hold operations up to the light to see what really makes sense from a customer perspective. If it doesn't, then we don't measure that exception anymore.

Results Reporting Plan

Anticipate how you would like to report results of the survey to the organisation – by account manager, by business unit, by sector, by department and how these will be presented. You also don't want an individual within the organisation simply receiving a survey report that shows a poor result without a process that engages the individual in a meaningful discussion and a remedial plan.

David Thodey: We implemented an aggregate score for the whole company - it was Enterprise, Small to Medium businesses, and Consumer, and we aggregated the three into one score for the whole company. There was a lot of debate about that. We said: "we don't have to be right or wrong, but we don't want the enterprise group saying somehow that we dislocated the consumer group".

Achieving Robust B2B Survey Participation Rates

The customer participation level in a customer survey project is vital. The lower the participation the less reliable the results of the survey, but more importantly, the less engagement caused between the company and its key customers. Customers want to know that you care about them.

Colm O'Neill: I knew I couldn't control the survey score, but I could control survey participation, to an extent. Participation had two benefits, first of all it was within our control. The second thing is that in order to get our participation rate to 50%, everyone in the team was going to have to have a conversation with their customers. I felt that if we came out of the survey cycle with nothing other than everyone on the team presenting this programme to their customers, then our customers would know we were listening.

It's easy to understand why people often choose not to participate in surveys. As consumers we are bombarded with questions most of the time we purchase something. The surveys range from the basic NPS question through to long, tedious, and sometimes repetitive questionnaires. Survey fatigue is not uncommon.

Research on surveys by CustomerThermometer provides these responses:

When a company asks for my feedback, I usually....

- Answer, but only if it doesn't take much time – 46%
- Ignore the request – 45%
- Take time to answer thoughtfully – 9%

Have you ever abandoned a customer feedback survey before completing it?

- No – 33%
- Yes – 67%

The challenge for business-to-business surveys is that people tend to adopt their consumer stance without realising the importance of the B2B relationship between supplier and customer.

The participation and completion rates for your customer survey are pivotal in capturing quality information. If you are achieving only 10 -15% of desired responses, the data has limited value and people may question the validity of the results. Of course, an expectation of 100% participation is unrealistic, however somewhere in the range of 30% to 60% is achievable with the right approach.

Here are a few suggestions on achieving robust B2B survey participation rates.

Call it something else

It's not deceptive to call it a 'relationship assessment' and avoid the 'survey' word. In a B2B situation, what you are genuinely seeking is some candid information about the relationship between you and you customer.

Keep it short

Obviously one NPS question is a brief snapshot about perception in a moment of time. Most B2B customer surveys need several questions to elucidate the reasons behind perceptions. However, the greater the number of questions the higher the likelihood of dropouts, and the less time people will spend. They will usually answer one question in 75 seconds, 10 questions in 5 minutes and 30 questions in 10 minutes (Source: SurveyMonkey). We suggest about 25 questions maximum (9 minutes).

Explain the Value

B2B relationships are two-way streets. Sure, there's real value for us to glean insights into customers perceptions so that we can improve our competitiveness, but there's also real value to the customer in achieving their own business goals with our help. Sometimes they don't understand this, so it's the role of the CEO and the account manager with a phone call, email and invitation letter to convey the value and that it is of strategic importance.

Don't do it too often

B2B transactions are likely to be multiple throughout the year, so you don't need to survey the customers views in depth on every transaction, or every week or month. They will feel as though they are being used if you seek responses too often. We like to assess trends, but in reality, you are unlikely to be able to correct major operational deficiencies inside a year. Once a year is enough, but make it regularly once a year so that they get into the rhythm.

Give Feedback (Close the loop)

Put yourself in the customer's position. The same old questions arrive every few months and annoy a busy person. They seldom hear what the supplier has learnt from the surveys, let alone what it will mean for them. You can't expect people to be loyal survey participants unless they understand what their contribution has meant. Closing the loop with feedback shows that you are serious about their issues.

Be Professional

A 'home-grown' survey might be easily concocted but it's usually obvious to the participant. If possible, use a professional customer survey firm and ensure that the questionnaire is derived from a research-based model that underpins its credibility.

'Warm Up' the Contacts

An invitation to complete a survey should not come out of the blue. Ideally, it should be introduced by letter or by email from the CEO or Country Manager, and while a survey is 'live', the account manager will know to stay in touch with the client and urge them to complete the survey.

Repeat

Get into a rhythm where your clients and your sales/account teams know that every February or October (or whenever), the annual customer assessment will take place. Some companies have quarterly Net Promoter or Pulse assessments – but don't overdo the frequency. Your organisation needs time to put remedial actions into effect.

Here's an example from Deep-Insight of completion rates experienced across a large number of customer surveys.

Figure 9 – B2B Customer Completion Rates (Frequency Bands)

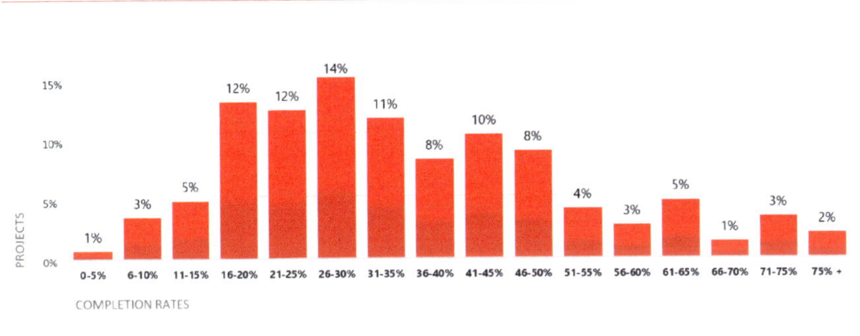

KPIs and Targets

At this early stage in the project it is worth anticipating how progress will be monitored. These KPIs and targets are likely to be included in a rewards strategy for employees.

The first (and most important KPI) is Customer Participation – that is the percentage of clients who actively participate in the customer survey (these can range from 30% to 60% depending upon how well the customers have been prepared).

The second KPI is overall customer score (whether it's NPS and/or CRQ).

The third KPI is about the results of the customer survey. How well is each part of the company performing in the key areas assessed by the customers. This may be with Net Promoter Scores and, preferably, scores related to deeper insights into the reasons for customer satisfaction or dis-satisfaction.

Example Project Brief

Background

At the recent Business Review meeting it was apparent that forward projections indicate that sales revenue growth targets will not be met in this financial year.

Reports from sales regions indicate a very competitive environment with expenditure constraints affecting key customers.

Aggregate corporate Net Promoter Score has fallen from +5 to -10 in 12 months. Some regions and some product groups are experiencing even greater falls in NPS scores.

There are some anecdotal reports offering reasons for this situation however there has been no investigation to identify why customers are reducing their purchases and as a consequence we do not have an action plan to address any issues.

Objectives

1. To improve the strength of our customer relationship to achieve a positive NPS this year.
2. To identify any customers who may be at risk of imminently defecting to competitors, and to act immediately to attempt to dissuade them from defecting.
3. To identify what products, services and in-house systems are causing customers concerns and to develop plans to remediate those that deserve priority.
4. To understand how effective our account management is and identify opportunities for improvement.

Scope

As there is a degree of urgency associated with this project it is proposed that we limit the customer survey to:

- The top 100 existing customers by revenue
- All branches in Australia and not off-shore
- All known contacts within the customer's organisation, not unknown contacts

The scope of the remedial actions that arise from the survey will be limited to those that can be executed within 12 months and do not require new CAPEX greater than $100K or OPEX increase greater than $100K. Remedial actions requiring greater investment will be listed for next year's budget process and treated as stand-alone projects.

Approach

A customer survey will be conducted on approximately 500 contacts within the 100 major accounts. The questionnaire will be in-depth to the extent that it provides information that enables the objectives to be met.

When the reports from the customer survey are available, regional meetings will address the findings and develop action plans that prioritise, estimate costs (including resources) and allocate responsibilities.

The CRM system will be upgraded to enable tracking, by customer, of customer relationship scores (including NPS) and the execution of the action plans.

Stakeholder Engagement

All departments within the company will be requested to nominate a representative to participate in a Stakeholder Analysis session later this month. The session will identify and prioritise the expectations of all stakeholders in relation to improving our customer centricity.

Chapter 13 – Tactical Planning

As we move from the Strategy phase of the project into the Tactics & Execution phase, the responsibilities should be transferred from the leadership team to a Customer Centricity Project Team allocated responsibility for delivering the customer centricity programme.

However, it remains absolutely vital for successful execution of the project, that the leadership team (including the senior leader) remain engaged in the project, are informed frequently about progress and are seen by all to be totally committed.

It may be difficult to convince senior managers to stay involved and not delegate, therefore you should position the customer centricity project as a strategic initiative and reiterate the insights to be derived, the likely outcomes and the expected benefits of the programme.

As Jim Collins expounds in his book 'Good to Great': "The key point ... is *not* just the idea of getting the right people on the team. The key point is that 'who' questions come before 'what' decisions – before vision, before strategy, before organisation structure, before tactics. *First* who, *then* what – as a rigorous discipline, consistently applied."

Chief Customer Officer (CCO)

We mention this role first as, if your company has appointed a CCO, this will heavily influence how your customer centricity project will be defined and delivered.

As Jeanne Bliss mentions in her book 'Chief Customer Officer – How to Build Your Customer-Driven Growth Engine', 2015: "The purpose of our work is to galvanise the organisation to deliver experiences that customers will want to have again – to earn the right to customer-driven growth."

Many large companies now have a CCO and it appears to be a growing trend. The important point is to ensure that the CCO is the 'facilitator' for the leadership and management teams to become more customer centric. The CCO should not be the repository where all customers issues are delegated to.

Selecting a Project Team

A project manager should be selected to lead the customer centricity project team and be accountable to the organisation's leadership team for successful delivery of the project. The project manager could be the Sales Director or Sales Manager or it could be a person specifically hired for the role.

It is important that the project manager is sufficiently senior in the organisation to enable them to participate in decision making with the leadership team and to engage with other senior managers whose business units will be involved with, and impacted by, the project.

Obviously, the selected project manager must have the time available to manage the project and an appropriate level of knowledge and experience within the business. At the same time, it is possible that a fresh pair of eyes will bring an unbiased approach to executing what will ultimately become a culture change project. We don't want a person with entrenched views of the business who will stifle critical analysis and avoid the challenges that will inevitably arise.

Another key person to select for the project team is an Administrator. Preferably someone who has access to the Customer

Relationship Management (CRM) systems and who has sufficient influence to work across organisational boundaries.

Other members of the team can be selected from the key stakeholders and will not only contribute to the planning and execution of the project, but also act as conduits to their stakeholder organisations. The number required will depend largely upon the size and complexity of the business and the scope of the project.

Responsibilities of the Project Team

It is highly likely the Project Manager will have been selected during the Strategy phase of the project and will have taken an active role, alongside the leadership team, and then, in Starting up the Project. Especially in writing the Business Case, the Project Brief and Selecting the Project Team.

When the project is approved by the leadership team the Project Manager and the Administrator will transition into this Tactics & Execution phase of the project. This initially means developing the Project Brief, Project Plan, Communications Plan and then managing the stages of the project. As the project nears completion they will precipitate the closure of the project and the Benefits Review.

The Project Manager and the Administrator will co-ordinate a series of project meetings commencing with the preliminary meetings with the leadership team, regular progress review meetings and follow-up meetings on action items agreed to.

Restructures

It's not unusual for an organisation to regularly undertake some degree of restructuring and this can often overlap with a customer centricity project. Rather than be viewed as a negative, customer surveys at this time can provide an ideal opportunity for a customer relationship temperature check.

Kathryn Whitehouse: We were all running on different systems. We had teams that just started working together. Relationships with the customers were broken in terms of the organisation's changes so the teams didn't know the customers, but we managed to go out to as many customers as we possibly could across the whole of the major and public sector organisations which is probably around about 2500 customers. About 20% of those make up 80% of our revenue. We got about a 15% response rate. What told a bigger story was that our customer relationship score from that survey was absolutely on its knees. You could've easily looked at that score and said, right let's pack up. We are never going to get anywhere from this.

The message here is the need to think long-term - commit to at least a 3-year programme to make a difference and have some consistency in the project team. Over the past number of years BT has gone through several re-organisations but the customer centricity programme has outlived them. Also, there never is a good time to start the customer centricity journey - you can always find an excuse not to start!

Initiating the Project

'Initiation' is the term used to describe the preparatory tactical work necessary to produce a viable plan for the project before execution commences. It includes:

- Risk Analysis

- Quality and Governance
- Controls, Reporting and Systems
- Communications Plan
- Project Plan and Resourcing

The purpose of planning in a customer centricity project is to translate the objectives defined in the Project Brief into an executable form. Essentially it is a description of what, how, when we are going to do it and who will do it (the 'why' and 'how much' were defined in the Business Case).

The sequence of creating these documents is deliberate. We need to anticipate risks, quality, controls and communications before we create the detailed project plan.

Risk Analysis

We should have captured any high level, visible risks in the Business Case and these now need to be transferred to our Risk Analysis. According to ISO 31000, (International Standards Organisation) risk is the 'effect of uncertainty on objectives' and an effect is a positive or negative deviation from what is expected.

In practical terms, we need to anticipate and document anything that could threaten the viability of the project. A very useful technique is to arrange a 'brain-storming' session with the project team and the key stakeholders and explore 'what could go wrong?'. Once the risks are identified we can record and analyse each risk in turn with a view to protecting the programme to the extent that is practical.

We should recognise that risks can be of three types:

- Risks that could affect the programme's ability to deliver the outcomes desired
- Risks that could affect the viability of the programme
- Risks that could affect the organisation (including reputational)

A Risk Register is a useful tool and we have provided a simplified version of this with some example risks. The Probability (or Likelihood) is an arbitrary score that might range from 1 – 'very rare', to 5 – 'happens often'. Similarly, Seriousness (or Impact) could range from 1 – 'minimal', to 5 – 'catastrophic'. The Risk Level, calculated by multiplying the two scores together allows the risks to be prioritised. You would act immediately if any risks emerge that have a level approaching 25.

Possible Consequences are, what would happen if this risk was to occur. We need to be pragmatic about consequences.

The brain storming team then needs to be creative about what Countermeasures (or Treatment) we can put in place to mitigate each risk. Countermeasures might eliminate a risk completely, or they might lower the probability or seriousness of a risk, or they might describe what we plan to do if the risk does occur.

Risk Register

Risk	Probability/ Likelihood (1 – 5)	Seriousness/ Impact (1 – 5)	Risk Level (PxS)	Possible Consequences	Countermeasure/ Treatment
CRM records inaccurate	4	4	16	Survey does not reach the target customer people	Update and purge the CRM system before survey
Account manager participation lukewarm	3	4	12	Poor customer responses. Low customer relationship scores	Revisit account manager briefings. Revise incentive plan. Consider restructure
Customer response rates low	2	3	6	Validity of surveys diminished. Opportunities for enhancing relationships reduced	Revisit customer communications. Re-activate account manager visits to customers

We should recognise that many of the countermeasures and treatment that we have identified should now become action items in the Project Plan.

The Risk Register is a 'living' document that should be updated regularly as the project is executed and new risks appear (and old risks disappear).

A diligent leadership team overseeing the customer centricity project, will want to see that risk management is being done routinely and will expect any high-level risks to be escalated to them for assessment.

Quality and Governance

Quality

The Oxford dictionary defines quality as 'The standard of something as measured against other things of a similar kind; the degree of excellence of something'. Quality can have a multitude of meanings, but here we refer to the quality of execution of the project.

No-one wants to be involved in a project that fails, but there are inevitable compromises that arise and being aware of their implications is important for both the project team and the leadership team.

Figure 10 – Quality, Time, Cost and Scope

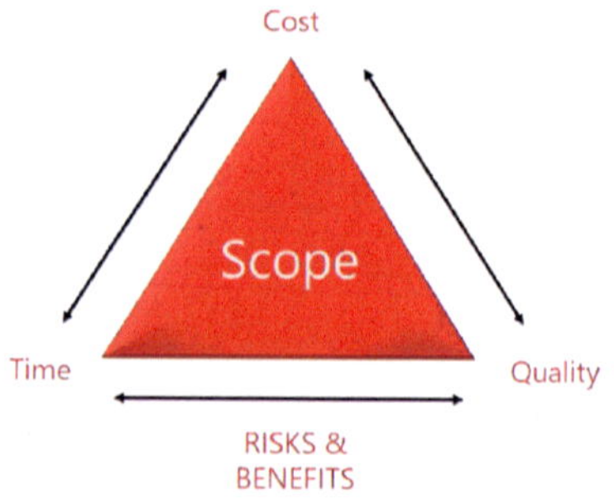

Figure 10 represents the nexus between quality, time, cost and scope. If the budget for the project is too small or reduced we may have to compromise on quality, time and scope. If the timescale for delivery of the project is too short we may have to compromise on cost, quality, scope. If the scope of the project is changed, there may be a consequent impact on cost, quality and time. Finally, quality (of project execution) could range from a shoddy, half-baked execution through to a gold-plated approach. Either extreme could adversely affect cost, time and scope. All of these are compromises and are likely to flow on to changes in risks to the project and possibly affect the ability to deliver the benefits.

Eamonn Galvin: The principle still holds that having a good, efficient, productive relationship between the customer and your Account Manager is very important, but typically, even in the offline world, customers are looking for value in the product that they're buying over and above the relationship with the key account executive. If you understand and can build the data that shows this, the value to the customer is the relationship, but it's also the other drivers of value, which include the quality of the product, or the range of services that are delivered by the product, or the value that the product delivers to the business, that are actually the key drivers of the relationship.

Governance

We anticipated the need for governance in Part III (Strategy) because it must commence at the leadership level. Now, in devising our tactics, we need to plan for governance actions in our project. It's worth noting that governance is likely to be a suitable countermeasure for some of the risks you have identified.

The Governance Institute of Australia states that: "Governance encompasses the system by which an organisation is controlled and operates, and the mechanisms by which it, and its people, are held to account. Ethics, risk management, compliance and administration are all elements of governance."

In a customer centricity project we recommend that the leadership team assign governance oversight responsibility to a senior manager who is not directly involved in executing the project.

The areas of governance to be monitored include:

- The ongoing viability of the business case (including realisation of benefits)
- The alignment of the project with corporate strategies
- The achievability of the project plan including expenditure plans and resource allocation
- The level of collaboration between the various parts of the organisation
- The success of the project in achieving its targets (customer scores, survey completion rates, etc.)
- Any very high-level risks
- The potential for, or occurrence of, attempts at gaming the customer survey process

This infers that the governance role is a form of project assurance and provides a mechanism for escalation to the leadership team if an exceptional event is forecast or is actually occurring, or if the overall programme is not being driven hard enough to achieve its targets.

The most practical prevention of 'gaming' is to ensure there is a clear set of rules in place during the phase of identifying the customers to be surveyed and the individuals within the customer organisation. The validity of the customer survey list is critical to achieving the integrity of the survey.

Mairead McSweeney: I was able to determine over a couple of surveys that there was a discrepancy and sometimes not the same customers were included in the survey. We had a monthly governance meeting with the leadership team, and I presented: "this is our proposed list of customer contacts; these are the changes from the last survey". The list was requested by the account manager and if there were any additions or any subtractions, or any changes in the contacts, I would ask why. Give me a business justification for the change. Their manager would sign off, and then, at the monthly governance session, I would present the adds, moves, and changes. I recommended which changes go ahead and which not. There were some account managers who just rolled in behind it, because they would see the benefit. And not only that, they would see that it's reflected in their Pay Plan. They wanted the programme to succeed. Others felt: there's no hiding anymore.

Systems, Reporting, Data Security and Crisis Management

The systems and reporting required will be unique to each company and should be identified within existing corporate procedures.

Systems

In the customer survey stage of a customer centricity project, access to accurate customer information is crucial. This is usually where a Customer Relationship Management (CRM) system is the essential tool. Unfortunately, many CRM systems have struggled to meet organisation's expectations.

In 2018 Gartner reported: "Customer relationship management has overtaken database management systems as the largest software market. By the end of 2017, worldwide CRM software revenue had reached $39.5 billion."

These are some of the main reasons for CRM failure:

- Data is not current and is not updated
- Lack of user adoption

- Thinking it's just a technology solution
- Not putting the customer at the centre
- Lack of training
- Too many bells and whistles
- Business and tech teams don't work together

For an effective customer survey it is vital that a complete and accurate CRM database be available – otherwise the customer centricity project will falter at the first gate.

Kathryn Whitehouse: Getting things automated quicker has really helped us because it makes the data very visible, and very manageable. For example, we ask the teams to deliver a brief to the customers before every assessment which aims to engage them, review progress with them and demonstrate our absolute commitment to this process. Then again after their feedback to review comments and scores and develop a personal plan to action the insight gained. We've got a stamp on the CRM system to report its been delivered, we've got a stamp to say that they've said they've done the follow-up and we've got a stamp to say we know that every customer has had an email from the boss before we issue to the survey. We are also now at the point where we can tell, in number of days, how many days it has taken us to go back and review with the customer. The actions that are agreed with the customer are part of the closed loop process.

Reporting

In terms of reporting results from surveys, it is crucial that the information be available in both a structured format for analysis by whatever filters were selected (geography, department, decision makers etc but also in a raw form so that future reports and analysis can be derived.

David Thodey: We put in place a data analytics tool that you could then drill down to the most remote Telstra shop. Every morning I could tell you by product, by channel, by process what the previous day's NPS score was and we could go down to every shop, to the extent that every individual would get a score the next day. It was a text message daily, weekly, monthly, quarterly, and annually. It was instilled in the very fabric of who we were.

Peoplebank is a 30 year-old Australian company that specialises in recruitment for the IT sector. It places 6,000 candidates each year across Australia as well as in Hong Kong and Singapore. Its CEO Peter Acheson is passionate about his customers and has his finger on the pulse on a daily basis. Literally.

Peter Acheson: We measure NPS online and real-time. Right now a contractor could be being sent an email about their experience with Peoplebank. If the experience wasn't a good one, and you're a detractor, the branch manager gets emailed that immediately and will phone the detractor and talk to them about what the issues were and to try and address whatever the shortfall was. We want to know what are the three or four things that are being talked about by the promoters and what are the three or four things that are causing people to be detractors.

Reporting progress is essential to the monitoring progress and generating momentum.

Colm O'Neill: We started on what was a really challenging journey. I kept on the MD's case saying, "We're not moving this thing forward. People aren't taking it seriously enough." We had this fake shock of "Oh. This is terrible," but no one actually doing anything different. Then we introduced a new report with a Top 10 analysis. It was brilliant, easy to understand and showed that we were delivering some of our worst service to our biggest customers. It was really powerful. We were able to communicate this to the broader organisation and say, "Okay. We're struggling to move the whole thing forward, but here's the Top 10. Here's where nearly 30% of our entire revenue for this business comes from, and we're giving them worse service than we give some of the companies that have no real business with us." It was an undeniable fact, it created urgency and that started to give us a momentum.

Data Security

It is crucial to ensure secure access to customer information and that the organisation abides by all relevant data protection and GDPR regulations (EU General Data Protection Regulation) and the ISO27001 information security standard.

Crisis Management

There should be a plan in place to deal with possible negative stories in the media. This plan should include the identification of a crisis coordination team, a plan to ensure timely and appropriate responses to negative press and regular internal briefings about the procedures for implementing a damage control plan.

The best CEOs are the ones that come out and say "our service isn't good enough, which is why we're putting this customer centricity programme in place".

Communications Plan

A core function of a successful customer centricity project is communications. This is best delivered through a visible thread that starts with an enthusiastic and committed CEO, through a supportive leadership team, a dedicated Project Team, to involved and loyal staff members and ultimately to the contacts in customer organisations.

One of the things that BT did very well in its CX programme was internal communications. Visit BT Centre in London and you will find customer quotes on the walls of the offices. Equally important in a geographically-dispersed organisation like BT, Colm O'Neill held regular video conferences with his extended teams where he would highlight recent client achievements and discuss customer-related targets for the coming six months.

> Kathryn Whitehouse: To succeed in delivering a customer focus project you need several things. You need your boss on-side if you're going to have a hope. The second thing is don't under-estimate the fact that you're running a process, and if you run it well and teams execute it well, it will work without a shadow of a doubt. The third thing is communications. Communications will change the culture and the visibility, especially in dispersed organisations.

A Communications Plan is an important part of a project's execution. As a living document, it defines all internal and external communications, clarifies the project and the organisation's priorities, target audiences, resources and staff assignments.

The purpose of the Communications Plan is to:

- To help us achieve our objectives
- To engage effectively with stakeholders

- To ensure people understand what we do
- To change behaviour and perceptions where necessary.
- To demonstrate the success of our work

The activities within the Communications Plan should support the organisation's overall Communications Strategies. It should set measurable goals in order to know when they have been achieved and be able to gauge the progress along the way.

It should develop key message points for the organisation's spokespeople to use when they talk with the staff, stakeholders and customers. It should also identify the communications materials (collateral) to be used and even provide templates for the core communications methods associated with the customer centricity project.

Communications tasks, responsibilities, budgets and timing should be included within the overall Project Plan. These should encompass

- Calendars of events, timelines and priorities
- Assigned responsibilities to lead and support staff, giving each a list of specific tasks
- Review progress and enforce or revise deadlines
- Holding people responsible for completing communications

Anticipate Your Audience

This is really part of stakeholder engagement that we suggested should commence in Part III – Strategy, but now it's essential to consider who and what is to be communicated. Think broadly about who your stakeholders are. They might include:

- Customers
- Shareholders

- Management
- Sales people
- Operations people
- Administration people

Peter Acheson: Look at who your customers are. We think we've got three. A client who actually pays the bill, a contractor who works for us at a client premises, but who equally is very important to our business and a candidate who is a person who might be a member of the IT community who is looking for an IT job. Any one of these three people can be a client, contractor, or candidate, depending on what's going on in their life at the time. It happens all the time - we'll place a person into a contract role and several months later they're a client.

Example Communications Plan

				Interested Parties						
Information Required	Information Provider	Frequency	Method of Communication	Project Team	CEO	Survey Admin	Sales Director	Account Managers	Staff	Customers
Process for running the survey project	Project Team	Once	Briefing and email			√	√			
What and why we are doing this	CEO	Once	Email	√		√	√	√	√	√
Account Manager's role and importance	Sales Director	Several times	Face-to-face	√				√		
What and why we are doing this	Account Managers	Several times	Phone/ Email	√		√	√	(Ctrl)		√
Results Presentation	Project Team	Once	Face-to-Face		√	√	√	√		
Individual customer results	Account Managers	Several times	Face-to-Face/ Email	√						√

Themes

Many organisations develop a theme that underpins their customer centricity project communications. This provides a memorable identity that can consistently be applied across the organisation and externally to customers.

- BT Ireland called their programme: 'Customer First'.
- BT (UK) runs an internal programme called: 'Customer Ambassadors'.
- Telstra called theirs: 'Our Customer Connection'.
- Australia Post called theirs: 'Our Customer Commitment'.
- The title of this book (Customer at the Heart) was derived from the theme developed by Atos: 'Client At The Heart'.

Christine Corbett: We developed a theme 'Our Customer Commitment':

We called the programme 'Deliveries that make you smile.'

- We have an unwavering commitment to delivering services that give you more convenience, control and choice. We strive to:

- Help you to connect to others and the world – your way.
- Listen and respond to what you tell us.
- Provide you with products and services that you want and need.
- Make it easier to get what you need, when you need it.
- Meet your future needs.
- Do more than you expect.

This statement was displayed on the reverse of every staff member's ID Card and on our website.

Internal Meetings

Most of the organisations we have encountered who have successfully implemented customer centricity, have thoroughly engaged with their people. Part of this is a conscious 'culture change' strategy that we address in Part V - Culture & Change however it is so important that we need to address it as part of 'communications planning'.

Internal meetings (sometimes called Town Hall Meetings) are to inform staff about the decision to become customer-centric and to encourage their support and participation.

Christine Corbett: For our staff, we did what we call a 'toolbox talk' and we said, "Here's our commitment, how would you bring that to life? What does this mean to you? How would you live this? What would we see differently?" This was run at every facility and post office in the country.

Kathryn Whitehouse: Our process runs around four customer presentations, supported by a raft of internal communications. One presentation before each assessment and one after each assessment. The first is to take the teams through what we've done across the business and the progress we've made. It gives them areas to capture their own customers' feedback and to shape their action plans. The second is to share our results and talk about our commitments of what we're going to do. Internal communication is important because if we haven't resonated internally then the external communication would never get delivered. We've got the internal people picking up the customer presentations, and proactively taking those out and presenting them in a professional thorough, compelling way.

Communications to and from Customers

These can include a spectrum of communications ranging from group consultation to one-on-one meetings.

In the early stages of a customer centricity project it will often be useful to seek the broad views of customers and identify high level issues. The insights gained can guide the design and content of more intensive (and individual) customer survey.

Christine Corbett: We created an enterprise program called 'Deliveries that make you smile' where we pulled together 50 people including consumers, small businesses, merchants, drivers, retail staff, licensed post offices, people in finance and in our product group, and we worked with them to solve customer problems.

Timely and persuasive communications with customers to recruit their participation in a customer survey are vital in achieving a reasonable participation rate.

Kathryn Whitehouse: Recruiting the customers into the process included giving the teams the support in terms of collateral and information. It was also very much about our MD writing directly to customers and sharing the principles directly with the customers, talking about his personal commitment, his ambitions for the organisation, and his appreciation of their engagement in this journey that we're commencing together.

Project Planning & Resourcing

The Project Plan is at the core of a successfully implemented customer centricity project. It provides the detailed answers to the questions of

What? When? Who? and How Much? Once completed and verified, the plan should provide the realistic 'Timescale' and 'Costs' for the Business Case we developed during the Strategy phase.

Your Project Plan could cover all of the stages of the project, for example:

- Customer survey stage
- Urgent initiatives stage
- Culture change stage
- Long-term initiatives stage

However, as mentioned earlier, it is likely that the latter stages of a customer centricity project will not be visible at the time of planning the first stage.

The project plan should identify all of the tasks and include a schedule of events. These might include:

- Selection of accounts to be assessed
- Selection of contacts within each account
- Extraction and verification of customer contact details
- Design of the survey questionnaire
- Selection of filters for dissection of the data
- Data collection and analysis
- Progress reporting
- Presentation of results
- Issue resolution workshops
- Feedback to customers
- Review of outcomes

Joe Edwards: You need to have a plan, if you don't, you're going to fall flat. You need to be thinking, "What do I want to get out of this project?

What is it I'm trying to achieve, and who is it I'm doing it to?" Because, sometimes you can't do it to everybody. Therefore, be very clear about the target market or target set of accounts that you are trying to do this with, and then ensure that once you start, you've got the team and the resourcing in behind it that is going to follow through.

The example plan below is based upon a customer centricity project in which the survey is the primary focus.

Project Plan Example

Deliverables	Tasks	Responsible	Date Due	Budget
Preparation	Develop proposed customer selection criteria and reporting filters	Project Team	Week 1-2	
Meetings & Briefings	Approval meeting	Leadership Team and Project Team		
	Meeting with CEO & Sales Director to discuss project roles	Project Team		
	Engagement and briefing of survey consultant	Project Team	Week 2-4	
	Announce project to all staff	CEO		
	Brief Account Managers	Sales Director and Project Team		
Questionnaire	Design questionnaire and correspondence templates	Project Team, Survey Consultant	Week 2-6	
	Approve final questionnaire and correspondence	CEO and Sales Director		
Customer Data	Finalise customer selection criteria and expected reporting filters	Project Team, Survey Consultant		

	Extract customer data from CRM system and validate accuracy – make corrections as required	Project Team, Account Managers		
	Send customer data list to Survey Consultant in agreed format	Project Team		
	Survey Consultant to send back any queries on the data list	Survey Consultant		
	Close off on Final Data list	Project Team		
Communication Plan	Send introduction letter to all selected contacts	CEO	Week 6-8	
	Send briefing emails to all selected contacts and follow-up with face-to-face visits or phone calls	Account Managers		
Live Campaign	Final data list changes	Project team		
	Launch online survey campaign	Survey Consultant		
	Email reminder 1	Survey Consultant		
	Email reminder 2	Survey Consultant		
	Final reminder	Survey Consultant		
	Close online survey	Survey Consultant		
Reporting	Access to reports enabled	Survey Consultant	Week 8 and on-going	
	Provide survey report	Survey Consultant		
	Present results to leadership team	Survey Consultant		
Action Plan	Document the action plan, identify costs and resources, prioritise, allocate responsibilities	Project Team, Leadership Team		

Instant Responses	Respond to potential defecting customers	Account Managers, possibly CEO		
Close the Loop	Plan visits or phone calls to all participating contacts to advise results and action plans	Account Managers		
Next Customer Survey Cycle	Plan the next customer survey cycle	Project Team	Week 8	

Here's an example of a Gantt chart to visually represent the project and to track progress against schedule:

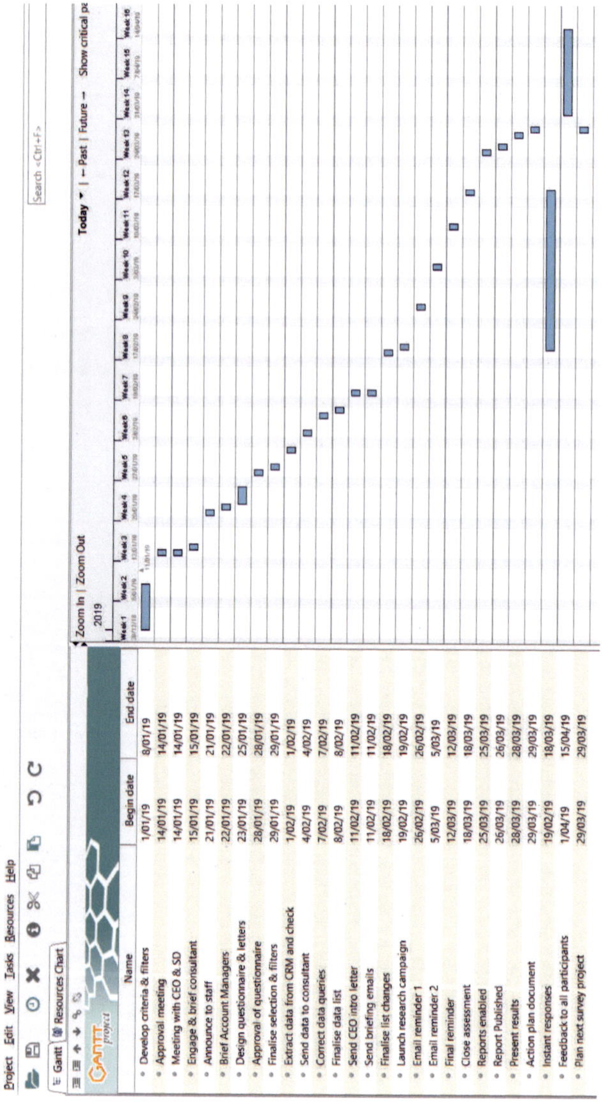

Name	Begin date	End date
Develop criteria & filters	1/01/19	8/01/19
Approval meeting	14/01/19	14/01/19
Meeting with CEO & SD	14/01/19	14/01/19
Engage & brief consultant	15/01/19	15/01/19
Announce to staff	21/01/19	21/01/19
Brief Account Managers	22/01/19	22/01/19
Design questionnaire & letters	23/01/19	25/01/19
Approval of questionnaire	28/01/19	28/01/19
Finalise selection & filters	29/01/19	29/01/19
Extract data from CRM and check	1/02/19	1/02/19
Send data to consultant	4/02/19	4/02/19
Correct data queries	7/02/19	7/02/19
Finalise data list	8/02/19	8/02/19
Send CEO intro letter	11/02/19	11/02/19
Send briefing emails	11/02/19	11/02/19
Finalise list changes	18/02/19	18/02/19
Launch research campaign	19/02/19	19/02/19
Email reminder 1	26/02/19	26/02/19
Email reminder 2	5/03/19	5/03/19
Final reminder	12/03/19	12/03/19
Close assessment	18/03/19	18/03/19
Reports enabled	25/03/19	25/03/19
Report Published	26/03/19	26/03/19
Present results	28/03/19	28/03/19
Action plan document	29/03/19	29/03/19
Instant responses	19/02/19	18/03/19
Feedback to all participants	1/04/19	15/04/19
Plan next survey project	29/03/19	29/03/19

Chapter 14 - Executing the Plan

It's worth making the point that the most important part of execution is the 'execution machine' – the person who runs the programme. All the other stuff (plans, reporting, progress meetings...) willingly happen if you have the right person running the show. The most successful project leaders we have seen have a sales background which gave the credibility, doggedness and passion.

Controlling a Stage

Controlling a Stage is the responsibility of the assigned project manager. It is essentially the execution of the project plan, stage by stage. It is about ensuring that the deliverables of the project, such as meetings, communications, surveys, action items etc. are delivered on-time, within budget, within scope and to the quality agreed.

Progress Review Meetings

Critical to successful delivery of a customer centricity project is tracking progress. As suggested earlier, systems should be in place to capture data on progress and to produce reports.

If deviations from plan are detected early enough, there will be opportunities to escalate the situation to the key decision makers in progress review meetings, and to decide what remedial action might be required.

Kathryn Whitehouse: The first 12 months was all around making sure that we had that customer recruitment in place. Really driving the response rates with the right customers. We've got a very robust daily reporting process around making sure that we've got a really high level of visibility. One of the most important things that you will do for this programme is communicate well. Then we set up the process of making sure that we were reaching out to customers and we were getting a response rate. As the responses came back in, we had a robust process to go back out to the customers, review the feedback and talk about their perspective.

Assessing the Customer Survey Results

As we have emphasised, a customer centricity project must be based upon well-surveyed facts – not assumptions, opinions or hearsay. The only practical way to obtain those facts is through a well-designed and managed customer survey project.

These are the categories of information that can be gleaned from such a survey programme.

- Net Promoter Score results – propensity to recommend
- The organisation's perceived Strategic Position (Uniqueness)
- Customers' view of the supplier (Ambassadors, Rationals, etc.)
- Strengths and Challenges
- Customer Relationship Quality – an aggregate score based upon trust, satisfaction, commitment, solution, experience and customer service
- Benchmarking against other 'Unique' companies

It will also be important to dissect the results as follows:

- Results by filters (geography, division, customer type etc.)
- Results for individual account managers

These are some of the traditional ways of analysing results but don't limit your analysis. For example, one of the most useful insights can be an analysis of which accounts or contracts are coming up for renewal or re-bid. A company's overall NPS scores might be good but if a couple of key strategic accounts are scoring poorly AND they are up for renewal within the next 18 months, then there is a major commercial risk that needs to be highlighted to senior management.

Another useful way of analysing the results is to split the scores by respondent type - Decision Makers, Influencers and Operational people, for example. We often find that Operational contacts have a very different perspective to Decision Makers because they are working at the coalface of service delivery. It's important to know if the relationships with these different types of respondent are consistent or not.

A valuable part of in-depth customer survey is to ask for verbatim comments from the participants. Questions, such as these, can provide extremely valuable insights:

- What is the supplier's single greatest strength?
- What is the supplier's single greatest weakness?

Capturing, Defining, Prioritising and Allocating Action Items

As we progress through the execution of the project, and particularly as we receive the results of survey surveys we will, as intended, identify a number of issues that affect our customer relationships.

The 'capture' process deserves some discipline so that all issues are recorded, and subsequently dealt with. This can often be accomplished within a CRM system, or more commonly by creating and managing a spreadsheet-based Issue Register that also becomes an Action Item mechanism. This is an example of an Issue Register:

Number	Issue Type	Description	Source & Date	Impact	Priority	Decision & Date	Action Allocation & Date	Status & Date Completed
16	Sales	Price lists are outdated	DT Jan	L	M	Update Jan	Mktg Jan	Done Feb
17	Ops	Deliveries consistently late for one customer	AC Feb	M	H	Track delivery	Ops Feb	Pend-ing

One of Kathryn Whitehouse's team at BT made an interesting point: it's only now (after 3 years) that all of these actions and processes have been embedded into Business As Usual and everything is now running as a well-oiled machine. In the early days, it was hard work for the customer centricity team to get things done, constantly reminding other people what to do and by when, cajoling, encouraging, supporting and administering the odd beating!

Kathryn Whitehouse: From an 'Inner Loop' perspective, which is what we call the activity our account teams undertake, we've transformed from a solely account management process to include Service Management and Contract Management. We've taken that process into our CRM systems where it's got a very high level of management visibility.

Closing the Loop with Customers

Feedback to customers is often called 'closing the loop'. It is possible that during the survey phase you will receive some very negative responses. These could give warning of imminent defection of a customer. It is prudent to have a pre-planned response mechanism in place at this early stage. This might include immediate contact by the account manager, the sales director and/or the CEO. It will also likely require a process for rapid fault correction if the customer's complaint is valid.

David Thodey: We wanted to use customer centricity as a driver of change and to make it a closed loop process, so that if we did a survey you and you said "I'm not happy", within 24 hours, we'd get back to you.

Mairead McSweeney: Most importantly, talk to your customers. That external piece where you say: "Thank you so much for taking the time to fill out the survey. This is what we think you've said, so we've heard you. This is what we're going to do about it." And then later - we've done this.

As we have stressed earlier, it is essential for those staff in contact with customers who have participated in a survey project to follow-up to convey our gratitude for their advice, what it means to us and what action items are relevant to them. This 'closing the loop' will not only fulfil the expectations of customers (in relation to the survey), but also encourage their participation in the next survey.

Mairead McSweeney: What I did notice through interviews with individual account managers, was that they would take the survey results to the customers, but they couldn't demonstrate to me that they actually spoke to the customer about the results. It's important to close that feedback loop. We know that only a small number of companies go back to customers and just say; "we've heard you." An even smaller percentage say; "this is what we're doing about it." And even less will say "we've done it, and this is the difference that we believe it's made, can you confirm?" We held our account managers accountable for actually telling our customers about the programme. We found that some of our customers were completing the survey and there was no response in certain areas by the account managers. Not closing the loop. Not getting that extra feedback from the customer. Not demonstrating we've heard what you've said, this is what we're going to do about it, and we'll tell you when we've done it.

McSweeney then explained how her boss Colm O'Neill got personally involved in closing the loop for the poorest-performing customers.

Mairead McSweeney: For the customers that scored us as the bottom 10, our MD Colm O'Neill went to meet the CEO of every single one of them. And that was followed up very quickly by the account manager or the sales director going in to meet their peers and reinforcing the message that: "we've heard you; this is what we're going to do about it". For some of the very poor scores, our MD followed up again on the next survey. He was looking at the journey, the survey-on-survey movements.

Chapter 15 - Completing the Project

Project Closure

It is tempting to consider a customer centricity project as never-ending, however it makes a lot of sense to consider each customer centricity project as one component of a customer centricity programme (that in itself should be never-ending).

A customer centricity project is likely to be an intensive period of involvement for many people within your organisation, and a favour sought from the customers being surveyed.

It is vital that real value be gleaned from the insights obtained into customers' views of the relationship.

When the results are available it is important that several layers within the organisation analyse these with a view to identifying issues that underly the reported results. The issues are likely to include cross-boundary problems and possibly entrenched stances and obstinate challenges. It is probable that not all issues can be addressed in the short term, so a prioritising system that considers effort and cost implications is desirable. However, it is also important to identify some 'quick wins' that can be made visible to customers so that their contribution to the programme can be seen to be worthwhile.

After the survey programme it is highly desirable to assess what has been achieved, particularly the consequences of issue resolution, and to endeavour to measure the achievement of the objectives.

Follow-on Actions & Joint Action Plans

This is where the evidence obtained in survey is converted into a prioritised set of solutions and action plans designed to fill the gaps identified. There are numerous client centricity tools, initiatives and programmes that can be tailored to suit the needs of the organisation. Here are a few examples:

Customer Journey Mapping Project

A project that identifies and evaluates the various touch-points that a customer is likely to experience with your organisation. It captures every facet from the initial search for a product, comparing suppliers and products, purchase, delivery and support. Includes on-line, social media and face-to-face interactions.

Voice of the Customer through Employees (VOCE) Project

A project that enables (and entices) employees to capture insights into customer reactions. These insights may be positive or negative comments about products, services or customer service. They can reveal competitive information, future purchasing intent, new product/service needs, strategic directions, company image and reputation. It is usually supported by an on-line VOCE capture and analysis tool.

Programme of Joint Customer Innovation Projects

A programme where employees (from across all functions) participate in facilitated innovation workshops where the primary focus is upon improving customer's experiences. Innovations can include new products, changes to customer interaction methods, changes to systems, changes to policies.

Joint Action Plans

A Joint Action Plan is a document that captures the meeting of the minds between a supplier and a customer. They develop trust through mutual accountability, knowledge and collaboration. The process of development is an open exchange of information, from both sides, on future directions, innovations, strategies and value. They usually include the terms of reference upon which a partnership is based for current and future business opportunities.

Kathryn Whitehouse: We're committed to drive those improvements through at an individual level. We go back to the customers, review our progress and then formally ask for their feedback again six months later. That cycle of feedback; action, review, and update has now been continual for nearly three years, before and after every customer assessment it's very much in everybody's faces on a daily basis but the ongoing focus throughout the year is equally important.

Evaluating Benefits

In the early part of the customer centricity project (in Part III – Strategy) we developed the Business Case that justified the project. The Business Case articulated the key benefits to be gained from adopting customer centricity within the company. As we close the project, we should endeavour to measure the achievement of those benefits.

In our example project we expected that the project would deliver an increase in net profit from 6% to 7% in the first year and an improvement in employee job satisfaction from 70% to 80% (as measured by the employee climate survey). The achievement (or otherwise) of these benefits should now be presented by the project team to the leadership team – remembering that in many instances the benefits may not necessarily be realised in the first year. Culture change is a slow process.

'Benefits realisation' should thereafter be on the agenda of all regular leadership team meetings.

Chapter 16 - Account Management

This book is not about account management. However, during the interviews we conducted with senior executives from companies who have successfully implemented customer centricity projects, we found (unsurprisingly) that effective account management was inextricably bound into customer relationships. We have therefore included some insights into this key component of customer centricity. Please also note the implications of account management at a strategic level mentioned in Chapter 2.

One important message was that successful account managers are always customer-focused and the selection of the right person for the job should include these characteristics: Friendly, good interpersonal skills, a little aggressive, quite competitive and with the resilience needed to cope with reasonably frequent rejection.

The account manager should not only be interested in people, but also develop an avid interest in the business of their customers. They must be able to represent the customer back into their own organisation and own the customer's problems that their company is exhibiting.

It's always a challenge for organisations to select and develop the right talent for the roles of account manager. It would seem that 'grow your own' with training and mentoring is often a successful approach.

The company must back the account manager totally. You cannot hold an account manager solely responsible for the relationship. They must be backed by support and resources that are needed to solve problems and further develop the relationship with innovation and better service.

Eamonn Galvin: Organisations need to provide direction or support to account executives so that they can deliver a high level of service in a more consistent and repeatable way. Even understanding the value of the account executives starts you on a journey of understanding how to provide them with the right tools and insights. How do you leverage the tacit knowledge of a high performing account executive and take that knowledge and insight, apply drivers to it, and move more of your account executives to that level?

That's where you do your ratings on your account executives and you can clearly see the high performers. People would look at those high performers and see a certain type of behaviour, but not necessarily understand what it is they're actually doing that makes the difference. Year on year, they're winning the awards for being the consistently the best account executives. How do they spend the time with the customers, is it the quality of time or is it the service they deliver?

In Chapter 9, we discussed Colm O'Neill's views on the role of the account manager and how strong account management is key to turning a supplier relationship into a partner relationship. O'Neill went on to share a couple of anecdotes with us about an excellent, if slightly unorthodox, account manager that he once worked with.

Anecdote 1

Many years ago, there was a mainframe sales executive (John) with a large IT company who did a deal with a large public sector customer to upgrade their computer system. The upgrade was hugely valuable for the whole company. It was literally the difference between the business unit doing its annual target or not.

After the order was placed, the customer called John back in to say that he had not got the necessary approvals and had to cancel. John went back to the business to explain this, and the MD for the business said, "We have a signed contract from them. The deal is done. We're not backing off. It's too late." John went up against the MD and demanded the order be cancelled. He said, "there was no way I am going to have a customer of mine exposed in that way". Now, you can have different opinions on John's behaviour, but that sale was cancelled. John protected his customer. Later I worked with John when I was at another company and he was selling millions of euros of IT systems to that same customer year after year. They trusted him with everything. He got more out of that customer than he ever would have, had he not made that earlier decision. Those experiences really give you a solid connection to the role that customer-centricity plays in turning decisions into financial value.

Anecdote 2

John was trying to get a customer to commit to a large order. The customer was saying "We understand the project, but we still have some questions and concerns. We'll go through these and we'll be back to you to get these done." John just said, "No, we're going to sit here now, and we're going to sort out all your questions, or I'm never coming to talk to you about this project again. Seriously, we've been in and out of here for months. I'm not wasting any more of my time on this. I don't think you should waste any more of your time on this, unless we can sort these things out now." The embarrassed customer said, "Okay. Let's work through it." John wrote all the questions on the board and we all sat there and pulled some technical people in. John was saying, for every question "Can we get that question answered?" so we went off to see if we could get it answered. Over three hours we answered all the questions and shaped it up. The customer was saying, "I don't know if I can make the business case fly for this" so, we got some of the finance people in from his team. We worked on the outline business case. John said to the customer "Have we got everything now" and the customer said, "We do. I think we have everything to take this forward. I'm going to need to put this into a paper, put it up, and get it signed off." That was high risk in the extreme and I was the most uncomfortable I've ever been in a meeting. We met again with the customer a week after it was signed off. The customer said, "John. I really appreciate you doing that to me. Things don't happen in here unless people make them happen, and you made it happen. We will be a better organisation for implementing this project. I really appreciate you forcing us to work through these issues to implement that process." Nothing happens until someone makes a sale, that goes for the selling and the buying organisation.

Summary of Part IV

- Tactics are about transforming strategy into an executable project
- Starting up a project includes developing a Project Brief and appointing a Project Team
- Initiating a project means preparing a risk analysis, considering quality and governance, anticipating controls, reporting, systems, developing a Communications Plan and a Project Plan
- Executing the plan means to follow the Project Plan and deliver all that is expected while reporting progress, assessing results and capturing action items. It also means closing the loop with customers
- Completing the project involves closing the project, ensuring actions are completed and evaluating the benefits derived from the project
- Effective Account Management is an essential element of a customer centricity project

Part V – Culture & Change

"I think as a company, if you can get those two things right — having a clear direction on what you are trying to do and bringing in great people who can execute on the stuff — then you can do pretty well."

– Mark Zuckerberg, CEO, Facebook

"If you always do what you always did, you will always get what you always got."

– Albert Einstein

"Everybody has accepted by now that change is unavoidable. But that still implies that change is like death and taxes — it should be postponed as long as possible and no change would be vastly preferable. But in a period of upheaval, such as the one we are living in, change is the norm."

— Peter Drucker

Chapter 17 – Where do Culture & Change fit in?

Deciding that customer centricity is a corporate strategy and then planning and executing a customer centricity project are very likely to generate short-term results. We observe that many companies that follow this path usually create a kind of euphoria in the organisation as scores from customer surveys improve, current customer problems are resolved rapidly, and customers are happier because someone is at last listening.

The risk is that the changes may not be sustained, and the results don't continue to improve. The enthusiasm wanes as the next year comes around and some of the inherent long-term limitations in the organisation continue - often because they are too large or complex to tackle.

The frequent cause is that we may have made some very visible positive changes, but the culture within the majority of the organisation hasn't changed at all.

'Organisational Culture' has many definitions. Here's a few:

- "The beliefs and ideas that a company has and the way in which they affect how it does business and how its employees behave" – Cambridge Dictionary
- "Organizational Culture is a group of internal values and behaviours in an organization. It includes experiences, ways of thinking, beliefs and future expectations. It is also intuitive, with repetitive habits and emotional responses. We also call it Corporate Culture. Organizational Culture is the result of a

perception within the company that its employees all share." – Market Business News

- "Corporate culture refers to the beliefs and behaviours that determine how a company's employees and management interact and handle outside business transactions. Often, corporate culture is implied, not expressly defined, and develops organically over time from the cumulative traits of the people the company hires." - Investopedia

Culture has also been regularly characterised as 'the way we do business around here'.

Many organisations attempt to measure 'culture dimensions' and there are numerous tools and consulting firms available to assist in this process. In this book, we are interested in one particular dimension of culture – 'customer orientation'. This means that if we were to interview every staff member in an organisation and rate them on their level of 'customer focus', we would have a clear view of how the customer fits into 'the way we do business around here'.

We are going to assume that your staff already have a degree of 'customer orientation' but that you can see that a significant improvement in this dimension would dramatically improve the sustainability of your customer centricity strategy.

The starting point is your statement of corporate vision. If it doesn't mention or allude to customers, then it's time it did. Here's some bad examples:

- Tesla: To accelerate the world's transition to sustainable energy.

- American Express: We work hard every day to make American Express the world's most respected service brand.

And some good ones:

- Caterpillar: To be the global leader in customer value.
- Amazon: To be earth's most customer centric company; to build a place where people can come to and find and discover anything they might want to buy online.

Once the strategic direction is defined and visible, it is then a matter of causing culture change. The rest of this Part is about how to do that.

Chapter 18 - Delivering Culture Change

From all that we have heard from the many interviews it is clear that a formal change management process is needed to ensure that customer centricity initiatives don't just wither on the vine.

There are a number of change methodologies that have emerged in recent years. In the past we have utilised all three of these but we decided to create a blend we have called the 'The Change Process'. We based it upon these three well respected approaches:

- Prosci ADKAR® Model is a goal-oriented change management model that guides individual and organisational change. It was created by Prosci founder Jeff Hiatt.
- John P. Kotter published an international best seller book in titled 'Leading Change' and introduced his 8-stage process for creating major change.
- "Switch – How to Change Things when Change is Hard" by Chip and Dan Heath.

We also recommend that the change needed to achieve on-going culture of customer centricity should, just like the customer centricity project outlined in Parts III and IV, be managed as a project because change is difficult. All our experience suggests that the journey towards customer centricity is a long one - years instead of months; a marathon rather than a 400m sprint - and a systematic approach is needed to make sure that momentum is maintained along the journey. We won't reiterate here the steps of managing a project, but we will utilise some of the methodologies available for delivering change.

Gavin Patterson: BT's corporate culture has changed over the 15 years, and it's even changed in my five years as CEO making sure that systems and processes are designed with the customer in mind first and foremost, particularly with forward - looking systems. So, it's a journey, as clichéd as it sounds, and it's a mindset as much as anything else. It means ultimately you need to find people who think customer first, who are absolutely determined to continue to improve the customer experience and ultimately will continue to find the educators.

The reasons for formalising a culture change project are:

- Change initiatives have a significantly enhanced probability of success
- Change initiatives are aligned with, and contribute to strategic goals
- Costs, effort and time are visible and controllable
- Resistance to change is minimised and engagement of participants maximised
- Risks of adverse consequences are avoided or reduced

Figure 11 – Delivering Culture Change

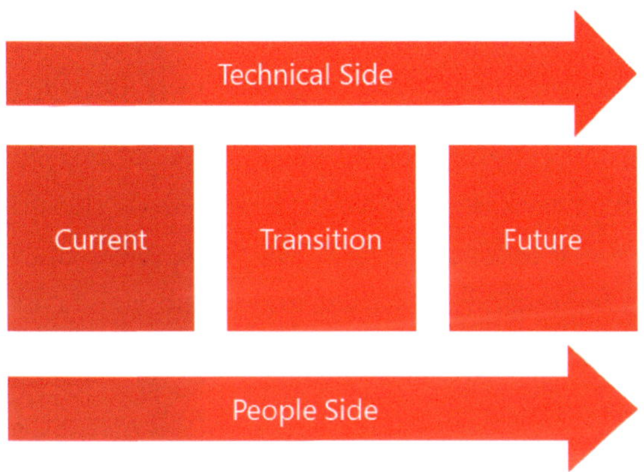

Any change project usually has two sides - the hard (technical side) delivering the practical aspects of change, and, the softer (people side) of change where we are sensitive to employees' feelings and where we recognise that meaningful change only ever happens when staff embrace it, because they believe it's the right thing to do. Both need to be in balance and compatible.

Peter Acheson: You've also got to communicate it at two levels. There's the rational, which is establishing the link, the scientific measurement. Then there's the emotional. They'll buy into it because they're passionate about it, and they want to feel proud of the customer service they're delivering. For any implementation of customer centricity, you can't just dictate it. You can even explain the logic of it, but you've also got to understand people's feelings.

The Change Process

The following guidance is intended for leaders who seek to achieve a culture change through working with their people (as opposed to announcing a change and expecting everyone to fall into line).

What we offer here is a synthesis of most of the elements of the methodologies mentioned, we've added some of the practical advice offered by our interviewees and we've applied our many years' experience in helping organisations implement significant change. We came up with a 10-step process.

1. Lead the change
2. Have a clear vision
3. Instil the values
4. Communicate and tell stories
5. Provide knowledge and skills
6. Motivate the people
7. Manage resistance
8. Innovate
9. Implement a Rewards and Recognition scheme
10. Sustain the change

1. Lead the change

People look to their leaders for direction. They want to see commitment from the top and at the same time they seek the personal touch of leaders who understand that change is hard. They expect their leaders to provide encouragement and recognition as they actively participate in the transformation of the culture.

It's why we included Part II – Leadership as a prerequisite to implementing customer centricity.

A sense of urgency is necessary, or the change process stagnates, however we must recognise that culture change is a not an overnight event. It is likely to take years.

Of course, providing resources and an achievable action plan are part of the leadership role.

Christine Corbett: From an executive level, the momentum needs to be measured, and it needs to be noticed, and critical questions need to be asked by board and management. If they're not asking the customer questions, then it's not a priority for the company. They need to be asking, why is NPS going up or down, what's happened, what can we learn, what can we accelerate ... and then it does filter throughout the organisation. If you don't have that commitment from the top, it doesn't matter how great the idea, there'll be another priority in the way.

Peter Acheson: The first lesson is that it is a journey. Cultural change takes at least three years. We've been on this journey on since 2009 and we're still on it. The second thing is that it's absolutely got to start from the top and you've got to stay committed to it. It can't be the latest CEO fad.

2. Have a clear vision

Most people, if given a clear vision of the future expected state of the organisation, will see the journey to that destination as a worthy goal. If they understand why we are on this journey, and the likely consequences of not taking the journey, they will align and contribute.

Clarity of purpose and consistent messages articulated by the leadership team are essential.

David Thodey: You can change the culture by putting the customer at the centre of everything you do and bringing the voice of the customer into the discussion and giving people permission to say; "if you serve the customer well, then you, will get a good profit outcome".

3. Instil the values

We talked about values in Part III – Strategy but it's worth revisiting these and recognising that people will begin to see that 'the way we do things around here' is changing.

The values identified and published by the leadership team may need to be adjusted to accommodate a new 'Customer at the Heart' culture in the organisation. It's also here that a theme might be applied to the customer centricity project. We talked about themes in Part IV – Tactics & Execution.

Gavin Patterson: In the same way that no system is perfect for every type of situation you need people to be able to focus on the values, fall back on the ethics of the company and the purpose of the company. Then when there isn't a system or procedure, they know that they have the authority to fix it. That comes from the words, that comes from the values and that sense of priority that comes through what you're talking about.

David Thodey: We'd always had the same values as most companies have; service, trust, respect, integrity, commitment. At about year three we actually created a completely different set of values that were things like 'say, you care', 'show you care' and that was also to each other. It keeps driving the standards inside the organisation higher and higher. Every conversation has got to be data driven around the customer. It drives far more change than you ever realise. And you also get ownership at all levels of the organisation.

4. Communicate and tell stories

It is obvious that staff members experiencing change to a customer-centric culture need to know what it means for them and what role they play in the transformation. We have covered communications extensively on Part IV – Tactics & Execution.

It became clear in our interviews that story telling played a big part in communicating successes and therefore indicating that progress was being made and people were motivated.

David Thodey: We did the classic 'tell your story' about why you work at Telstra and the stories were incredible. We asked for stories from the field engineers, who would do unbelievable things. They would bend over backwards for the customer. They were the heart of the company. We had 8,000 field technicians and 20,000 people in call centres. These people did remarkable work every day. To hear their stories and enabling them to do a job that they're proud of, is really powerful.

5. Provide knowledge and skills

Inevitably, with a culture change occurring in an organisation, there will be changes to procedures, business processes and people's jobs. It's important that we recognise these as needs for new guidance, training where appropriate and support mechanisms to help people adapt to the new ways.

6. Motivate the people

The topic of motivation is vast and there are many books available on the topic, so we won't explore this in any depth here. From Steve Chandler and Scott Richardson's book '100 Ways to Motivate Others': "Motivating others requires a connection to people's deep desires. It's not just about loading them up with a lot of how-to information. Transformation is more important than information. Action is everything. A great motivator of others will value testing over trusting."

The leadership team and their managers must understand that their people will experience strong positive and negative feelings about the changes.

Gavin Patterson: If people aren't inspired by it, if people aren't prepared to use their discretionary effort to go the extra mile, particularly when it comes to exceeding customer's expectation, it becomes impersonal. It becomes something where people are turning the handle only a little bit.

Peter Acheson: The piece of really critical information is employee engagement. We know that because what we're selling is intangible, invisible, can't be touched, can't be test driven, that what a client or a contractor actually is buying, is our people's passion, enthusiasm, and conviction about Peoplebank's ability to solve their problem. In the branches where we have the highest engagement score, we have the highest client and contractor net promoter scores, and we have the highest gross profit per employee.

Christine Corbett: Many of the process issues, which are often technology-based are in the back room, not front of house. How do you get those people in the back room on board to say, "we are actually working for the customer, too"? We set up a cross functional team that included people from the back room and we had people from head office, people from technology, people from finance all involved. They had a sense of ownership that makes that journey so much easier. At the end of the day, people want to do the right thing but they need to know what role they play. By articulating up that upfront and making it better for our customers, we had people throughout the organisation advocating for our customers. The back room want to know how they can contribute. So, their active involvement in the front line made a huge difference and they then became huge influencers to others.

7. Manage resistance

We need to anticipate resistance and be ready to counter any negativity that emerges. These are often the reasons why culture change can be difficult:

Perception	We see what we expect to see
	Failure to see the real cause of a problem
	Too narrow scope of a problem
	Not seeing all sides of a problem
	Not exploiting all the information that is available
Emotional	Risk-aversion - fear of making mistakes or failure
	Being in the dark - incomplete or contradictory information
	Preference for existing ideas instead of generating new ideas
	Not taking time for thinking - pressure to deliver results quickly
	Perceiving changes as a threat to personal status
Cognitive	The use of unfamiliar language and terminology

	Failing to apply agreed strategies
	Lack of complete and correct information
	Information overload
Cultural	Particular issues might be no-go territory in an organisation
	More focus than imagination - lack of creativity
	Believing that critical reasoning, objective analysis, logic, figures and facts are the only way
	Perceiving that intuition and fun are seen as sub-optimal
	Not challenging and overcoming traditions
Environmental	Lack of support
	People who try to stop or ignore the process
	Lack of management ability to accept criticism
	Managers who always know the answer – not listening

Mairead McSweeney: At the start there was a little bit of reluctance on: "Why am I accountable for all customer experience, including delivery, when I'm just here to sell?" But I really feel that after the first survey, where we demonstrated a huge leap in scores throughout the structure, through the mechanics, through the communication, and through the reward, people said, "right, this is worth it. I personally benefit from it, and the company's doing really well". It still took us a while to get some of the account managers through it.

Sue de Wit: A lot of people really didn't like it to start with because it felt quite confrontational. What the CEO did quite successfully was to be challenging and coaching, in terms of getting people to look at it quite differently. To look at the actions they were taking, and that needed to be taken. Look at it through the customer's eyes, and then look at it through the Atos eyes in terms of Customer First. It's not about how much more efficient can you make it to save money, it's about how efficient can you make it so that you can be more responsive to the customer.

8. Innovate

In any transformation of an organisation there will need to be changes to the way we produce and deliver our products and services. This means changes to Operations and Service in the organisation to better align with the new customer focus. Encouraging innovation, lateral thinking and finding ways to overcome barriers is essential.

David Thodey: They could submit process improvements to the central group to fix process issues. Or they could put through innovation ideas, which is doing things completely differently. And that would go to another group, who would say "Can we innovate our way out of a particular issue?". Sometimes people brought recommendations up and it just wasn't going to happen for a year so we tried to be as transparent and as straightforward as we could. For the age-old saying 'those people in Corporate', we tried to break those barriers down and just say, "we're not going to be able to fix that, so is there anything you can do to work around it".

9. Implement a Rewards and Recognition scheme

A change project needs checkpoints to measure progress and also to celebrate success along the way. We suggest that rewards and incentives should be part of the change 'package'. Some early wins in a change project will often gain attention and provide motivation for the ensuing change tasks. The topic of rewards and recognition is covered in Part III – Strategy.

What BT Ireland and MPS did very well was to recognise people's efforts - Colm O'Neill would personally call people who were named by customers for having done a good job and it had a huge positive impact on morale (at no cost).

Mairead McSweeney: We were highlighting some of the good work that was done and we had some really positive feedback about people across the organisation who have helped a customer, both from the account manager and the customer. And for the account team to see the field engineer or the service manager being rewarded and recognised for a good job that they did for their customer, that helped. Our ability to demonstrate to our people that this is what we're going to do, and we did it.

10. Sustain the change

There's always a risk that the implementation of the first stage, or two (or the first year) will be viewed as the end of the change process. Nothing could be further from the truth. We need to sustain the impetus or momentum of change. This is often done by re-setting the project objectives, planning for a fresh approach to communications, introducing new reward and recognition programmes, and engaging the leadership team to re-iterate the importance of the strategy and progress along the journey.

Gavin Patterson: Organisations have a finite amount of energy, and what you have to be able to find is the moments to sprint and the moments to really do the heavy lifting for just a couple of things a year. It means that things like continuous improvement around customer experience has to be a subconscious habit, because you need it 365 days a year. When it's been a top down edict, we've not got traction.

What we need is behavioural change. This is a way of working that you need to make just part of the way we do things around here. It's that self-propelling drumbeat, heartbeat of the organisation, you have to get right. Then you save the sprints for the moments of crisis, or the moments where you have to launch something in a discontinuous way.

Christine Corbett: Sustaining the cultural change is the hardest thing. It has to be top of mind and there's so many other things that can come along and get prioritised, so it's that relentless pursuit that is important. It's very easy to get excited in the beginning when there's something new but six months or 12 months later, it is hard to keep that excitement. Consequently, having some of the more tactical quick wins to maintain enthusiasm is really important, because the bigger, longer term strategic issues which are the game changers, will take longer. You need to have the buzz and the excitement throughout.

Managing Complex Change

This 'Managing Complex Change' model was created by Dr. Mary Lippitt in 1987. It simply recognises that change cannot be achieved piecemeal – it must be a holistic approach that addresses each step in a change process.

Figure 12 – Managing Complex Change

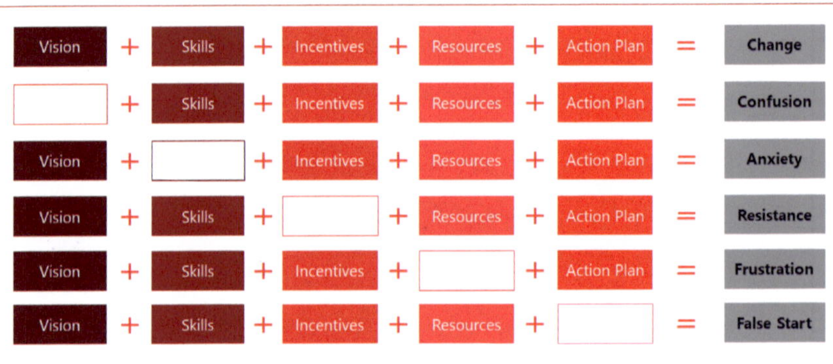

Summary of Part V

- A customer centricity project might achieve short-term changes, but if you want to sustain this success you need to embark upon a culture change project in parallel
- There are many change methodologies – select one that suits your culture
- Culture change needs to address both the hard (technical) side of change and the softer (people) side of change
- Deliver culture change through a series of steps that bring your people along the change journey – and then sustain the change into the future
- Complex change must be holistic

Part VI - Customer Stories

The purpose of these interviews with customers of BT is to show that all customers have their own unique sets of challenges and objectives and that it's the job of the supplier organisation and the account manager in particular to get to understand those particular nuances and position the supplier's products and services to solve a particular problem, rather than just trying to sell what they have in their kit bag.

Bob Brown's Story

Bob was Chief Information Officer for Manchester City Council reporting directly to the Chief Executive. He was responsible for the provision of, the support of, and the change of all technology for the Council. That included systems for internal operations and also for all 580,000 residents that use their services.

Within our organisation previous attempts to recognise how important and how strategic technology change is, and has been, and will be, were not well-appreciated at all. Whilst we have great-minded individuals, we had gone through a series of asking non-professionals to look after the technology function. Some of the decisions that were taken, from a professional technologist point of view, would have been questionable, but equally, the lack of investment had created what was essentially a burning platform.

Fundamentally this was not an internal customer-centric organisation. It wasn't providing reactive or proactive services in any way that would pass any form of satisfaction survey. Externally, those who provide services that we buy from the marketplace had actually forgotten who the customer was. We had to set about changing the internal and external perception of our services and setting the context of what was a very clear strategy of which we were expecting people to follow.

Now, once a quarter, I share my strategy and I ask suppliers for help to evolve it. I'm transparent in a way that we talk about where we're going to spend our money over the next two years so that our partners can build an account plan that's specific to our needs, not to their business model. Unless they're looking to support our city's direction, then they know, and we know, not to have those conversations and waste each other's time.

BT was a long-standing partner but a transactional relationship and certainly one that wasn't engaged appropriately and wasn't delivering value for money services. They had enjoyed a long-standing relationship with poor contracts in place on both sides that weren't being managed, and both parties were failing as a result.

We had to say to BT, "Look, these practices have to stop. These things have to change. We have to build an account management plan together that is going to change where we are, and if we don't do that, then let's help each other to part in ways that help each other, rather than continue to try and push water uphill, because you, as BT, don't appear to want to change and flex to our way of working."

I said to this supplier "I'm absolutely clear what my threshold is when you frankly annoy us when you introduce service failures and we have to issue contract breach notices. If you introduce failure into our estate, expect a call from my team." That's the negative side of it.

Equally, I want to give suppliers the opportunity of bringing forward ideas through innovation. "How do you know what good looks like from our point of view?"

Part of my organisation's strategy agenda is growth in terms of economic growth. The partners that we work with have to comply with something called social value, and we weight every contract issued to the marketplace against social value. It very much favours those organisations that are based here, or are prepared to be based here, prepared to invest in our locality, prepared to get to know us, to be on our doorstep, to go to our schools and to employ our local people.

It's also about how we introduce system-related change to provide benefits, rather than tactical change to drive revenue. Inevitably, both sides need to get value from the relationship. What I need to see much more of is the ability to use innovation to help us change fundamentally our systems, not just our technology process.

I would welcome the opportunity of having strategy days with conversations between supplier's account managers and my team, and to bring our joint leadership teams together at a senior level and identify innovation opportunities.

An effective account manager is somebody who bridges the strategic and the tactical elements of the account. Somebody who has the empowerment to be able to pull in other parts of their organisation, and to ensure that the customer doesn't see the cracks in the internal structure such that it's seen to be presenting joined up solutions.

Equally somebody who is purely sales-focused can never be a modern account manager without understanding what is important for their client, what their client's strategy is, and how they can align their account plan. I think every good account manager needs to have been a senior practitioner at some point in time.

BT have responded by completely changing the account model, changing the relationships that I have on the ground, or my team have on the ground, and they are delivering value, and that enables us to then score things very differently. Today we have a much more positive and proactive relationship in place.

I think to some extent they bought themselves out of a problem. There's been internal investment that has gone into this, which is disproportionate for their usual revenue models, and I think it's only possible that that situation has been allowed to happen because of how high the issue went within the organisation, how visible it was that those problems existed, and it's been a conscious ploy to get the support for Manchester City Council changed. I've had to educate BT along the way and they do appreciate more of the public sector's wider responsibilities than previously.

A good competitive example of customer centricity is ServiceNow who are really dominating where they're looking to sell their product sets. Their account management team see us on a very regular basis. We celebrate together, we go on journeys together that may not necessarily lead us to the outcome we set off at the start, but we're prepared to put some investment in that on both sides, and they're certainly bringing innovation in ways that other organisations haven't been able to do.

Lindsay McCaughey's Story

As Chief Technology Officer for Galliford Try, Lindsay has overseen the major project of migrating all IT services to a cloud solution provided by Microsoft. They needed a substantial technology partner to manager their business-as-usual IT services. BT (UK) was a possible contender for the partnership.

We were in a pretty bad place with BT, there was a new account team assigned who were trying very hard to make things happen. I will give them praise, however, they were sales guys.

Their ability to influence and persuade others to get us the service that we should be getting was negligible. At that point in time, even if I was in the position to select a partner, it would not have been BT.

I've dealt with BT for the best part of 35 years and the thing that's always cheesed me off with BT and what used to cheese me off with IBM, is that there's so many internal markets. Everybody wants to do their thing and wants to see their flags flown, but the customer was neglected.

You'd make a call requesting support and the system would throw it out to an engineer on second support. You don't hear anything. You're trying to request priority with no response in eight, nine hours. It just went into black holes, passed onto the wrong people and no-one wanted to take ownership.

We had a senior level contact and whenever you spoke to the senior guys the noises coming back were really positive and really strong, but it never played out at the grassroots level. We were dealing with many different teams and there was no single point of contact. Even when we were dealing with these people and logging calls you would think that everybody's working on it. You're chasing it up, "Look I've heard nothing in four or five hours." And nothing has been done – it hasn't even been passed on.

The sales guys tried really hard and sometimes they could pull a rabbit out of a hat, getting somebody aligned to fix the problem, but it was a very unsatisfactory relationship. It certainly wasn't a partnership, more of an old-fashioned, old tier type customer-supplier relationship. Somebody turns up and says, "Right. You must have this." As opposed to "Mr. Customer, what do you think you are trying to do?"

We ended up with a couple of spectacular failures which impacted Galliford Try for numerous days on end. One of the failures was when we lost internet connectivity for the better part of two and a half days. People were working off phones and off broadband just trying to get through to the internet. It was an appalling situation. The pressure from the executives back onto me and my CIO was phenomenal.

I met with the BT commercial manager and the account executive and I said, "All right. I ain't paying you another penny." I think I was withholding about one and a half million pounds.

BT Global Services changed to BT Public Sector and Enterprise and we started getting a different feel. Different types of people came in including a new Director of Client Services. I was expressing to him the problems and the frustrations I was having, and from that period, BT really did start listening and understanding.

We then received first line, second line, and third line support from a team who are all sat together and who could talk about our problems and priorities instead of getting lost in the huge BT machine and processes.

Since then, the account management team have been really positive for the first time since and we've actually started talking about new products.

We now have access to a more senior person and levels within BT who actually listen to you from a business point of view and service provision has improved. They said, "We understand your pain points, we understand your problems and we understand where you are coming from." Then we started working to put processes in place and managing the services. Even now, at a deeper level, the feedback of my engineers and my help desk staff is very, very positive. We now have joint meetings between help desk management in both organisations.

We are up for contract renewal right now and I would probably would have been going out to other parties were it not for the BT Director of Client Services.

It isn't just about the service, it's about responsibility. If a customer rings with a problem, 1: you need to take the problem away from them, 2: keep them communicated at all times, 3: go back with the answer that they need. If you do that, customer satisfaction goes through the roof because there's nothing worse than just sitting there not knowing if somebody's doing something or not, you fear the worst.

My advice for account managers is to understand what it is you are trying to achieve and not trying to force old-fashioned legacy products on us. Understand the suite of products that we've already purchased and how BT can then be a partner to help us leverage and maximise our spend in that space. Introduce the services that form a wrap around those.

From a services perspective what we need is much more proactivity. Look down the road in the next six months and saying, "All right, you know these products are coming to end of license in six or seven months' time and we need to start thinking about what we are going to do with them."

The problem we've got is that if people aren't going to be flexible enough and actually come up with fairly innovative solutions, it's going to be problematical. That mentality of silos in the product area still exists.

I think if BT really wants to enter the world of partnerships, what they need to do is come to me and say, "You've purchased these products and you're implementing them. We can bring you services to help you, as a partner." "We can lump these bits of product together to create a full solution."

I know the product stack has gaps in it, how do I fill those gaps? At the moment, I am doing that myself. They need to be quite bold and more innovative.

They also need to understand that our company is already invested. Where they are going to make their money is not by trying to sell us a product we already have but selling us a product that sweats the assets we've got and adds value.

They need to be thinking about who the big disruptors are, but they're not fitting that world of speed of change and fast-paced movement of the cloud. They're still offering the traditional five-year CAPEX-type product solutions. From the product side of it, they need a complete refresh and rethink.

Part VII – Outcomes & Learnings

- Atos
- Australia Post
- BT (Ireland)
- BT (UK)
- Ebay
- Peoplebank
- Telstra
- Toll Group

"If you believe in what you are doing, then let nothing hold you up in your work. Much of the best work of the world has been done against seeming impossibilities. The thing is to get the work done."

– Dale Carnegie

"Effective leadership is not about making speeches or being liked; leadership is defined by results not attributes."

– Peter Drucker

"What do you really believe makes a difference in the company? For me it's really clear. It's about customers and employees. Everything else follows. If you take care of your customers and you have motivated employees, everything else follows."

– Anne M. Mulcahy

'Outcomes' are usually defined as 'the resultant change derived from what a project delivers'. Outcomes lead to the realisation of the benefits expected.

'Learnings' are derived from the experience of implementing the project and delivering the outcomes.

Here we provide some first-hand descriptions of outcomes (with a few benefits also mentioned) and learnings from some of our interviewee organisations.

The core message is that this stuff is hard, but it's worth it in the end.

(Our apologies if we have repeated a few quotes here, but they are important examples of outcomes and learnings).

Atos

Sue de Wit: Everything we did started with 'Client At The Heart' and it was a huge influence on the rest of the organisation. That's absolutely key; if you don't have that very senior sponsorship to any change that you're trying to drive, it's just not going to work. What I would do differently is to have yearly big shakeups. Although we keep trying to introduce something new, and something different, I don't think it's necessarily been big enough in recent years. What's been far bigger for us is some of the non-client focused things and therefore our 'Client At The Heart' theme has faded. Maybe that's where we went wrong, it needs reinvigorating with a slightly new theme on it, a slightly new name, with a slightly different component in it to keep it in peoples' mind, keep it fresh. We stuck with the same theme. It would also be valuable to have greater input from the grassroots. As an organisation, what we don't do very well is listen to our own people at the sharp end.

Some of them have lots of brilliant ideas, and you do come across them when you go out to different sites. You hear about these things and ask; "That's great, why don't we do that elsewhere, why haven't we made this a much bigger thing?"

Australia Post

Christine Corbett: We measured first time delivery and net promoter score. In 18 months, we achieved a 6-percentage point increase in NPS and it continues to gain momentum. First time delivery increased to above 90%. We created an app that allowed our people to be positive advocates by capturing customer issues and setting up an accelerated workflow whereby both the customer and the relevant staff member were contacted within 24 hours. We also captured sales leads and importantly the app enabled staff to report safety hazards that might affect other staff or customers. They could take a photo with the GPS location attached and our OH&S team would be notified. Culturally it showed our people that we were serious about them and we're serious about our customers.

BT (Ireland)

Colm O'Neill: We experienced a massive improvement and step forward in customer experience in the BT Ireland business, we've completely turned the business around financially and operationally as well. The Republic of Ireland business was the most financially successful business BT had outside of the UK. The Northern Ireland business, which is part of the UK, on its comparators with the UK financially and operationally, was the most successful part of that business. Along with customer experience success came enormous financial success. Every time you go through those changes you get an increase in confidence in the philosophy that you make an organisation a customer focus organisation.

BT (UK)

Kathryn Whitehouse: The biggest learning from that process is, this will never end. As the customer feedback changes and as we improve, the customer's businesses changes and they need us to adapt. We've now moved from siloed service issues, to much more strategic, generic enhancements areas, or innovative relationship development areas with the customer. There is an ongoing cycle of improvement. The teams have embraced it in line with the leadership. When we started the process, at all levels in the organisation we had probably 20% buy-in to the process. We've worked hard to try and break down those barriers over the last two and a half years, we're now probably at 70% buy-in. That's probably 80% leadership focus, and 60% adoption across the team. Huge opportunities are still ahead, and given the progress that we've made, it's frustrating that there remain some pockets of resistance. We could go so much faster. You often hear "BT can never do this right" or "I'm going to take this back to the business." And I think creating the culture of 'We are the business' and with the right focus, with the right collaboration, with the right attitude, with the ability to open your mind to different ways of working, we can actually take ourselves a long way forward. I think focusing on what we can do, not what we can't do, has really helped the successful teams. When you take a bird's eye view over a period of three years there's a huge financial gain associated with the points improvement in our NPS score. The correlation is absolutely clear, as we've moved forward, we've seen our customer relationship score improve in-line with our profit improvement. For example, we calculate that the long-term value of a customer in sales revenue is about 75% greater from any customer that is Passive Plus. We estimate that we achieve three or four times returns, for moving customers along the NPS scale from top end Passives to bottom-end Promoters. One of the challenges is the cycle. You have to take time to take a step back and build these relationships to see the future benefits of them. You've got to be skilled at running your business, in terms of looking medium, short, medium and long-term opportunities.

Ebay

Eammon Galvin: The value of NPS is when you use it to challenge how you think about the initiatives you use to drive performance. For example, in eBay, when we tracked NPS on customer service we were lucky, because we had very large volumes. On a monthly basis we could have between 15 to 20 thousand NPS responses, which is a huge sample. But month over month that number was very consistent. The big learning was realising that unless you actually did something meaningful and significant that was right for the customer, the NPS number didn't change. At one point the customer service component of the programme was being delivered by a customer service agency in the Philippines. We tracked NPS daily with a large sample size and we began to see a decrease in the NPS. It was not because all the customer services were being done in the Philippines, what we found when we investigated it further, was there had been several communications outages in the Philippines, typically due to tropical storms. The 'aha moment' was realising that a tropical storm in the Philippines had affected the customer service for the individuals calling and this was reflected almost immediately in the NPS. The point is that if you are continuously providing a high level of service and NPS declines, then there is probably a root cause for decline. When people see fluctuations in NPS some of those can be due to sample size, etc., but you need to understand what the underlying reason is behind that NPS fluctuation. The important realisation is that if you're not doing things that the customer believes are important then your NPS will not change. As we implemented a series of improvements, we saw an improvement trajectory on our NPS. But then, as soon as the improvement delivery stopped, NPS went back and flatlined at its new base level.

Peoplebank

Peter Acheson: We recently held focus groups with a representative group of our contractors. There were two key messages: Firstly, they want to see consistency in terms of the personal service that they receive. They might have talked about great experiences that have created raving fans, but equally, there were some examples of where they were dealing with some part of the organisation where the experiences weren't as good as they would have liked. It's consistency in terms of service experience. The second key thing was that, in their minds, that we are a standout company in listening to our contractors. They don't get invited to participate in focus groups with other recruitment companies. In other companies, contractors are seen as a pain in the ass. So, that was part of our turnaround, in terms of the cultural transformation. These guys are actually our customers as well, and we need to treat them as our customers.

Telstra

David Thodey: We had some bad moments on the way but it sort of really rallied the whole organisation to come together. For the first two years we hit the target, and remember I was paid more on the NPS target than I was on the corporation's financial results. Everyone in the company was on some form of bonus. The third year, we missed the target. I got zero bonus, and everybody got zero in the company. We used a social media platform called Yammer, and it could show things trending in our social media, it really trended that day. Everybody came out - the engineers were blaming the sales guys, the sales guys were blaming the product managers, and then we said "hey guys, we're all in this together. We live or die together". And it brought the company together, in a way that I'm really glad about. Even though I didn't like not getting my bonus, they realised we were really serious about it. A four-year journey is hard, disciplined work. It's not friendly faces, doing smileys, it's hard re-engineering - it's disciplined and rigorous. Sometimes you can't make progress and you don't know why it's not moving. You've done things but you've got to keep asking 'why' and moving forward. It's a long journey. One pitfall is that people look for the sugar fix. It's not. This is not about making people feel happy. It's about deep re-engineering of the business and about using it for product design and driving process improvement. This is a significant transformation. We did perception surveys because one of the big things is reputation, and reputation is different to advocacy. There's a reputation score for every corporation in Australia and we went into the Top 100. Also, in 2014, we were voted the most respected company in Australia. Our EBITDA improved by 35%. Our share price started at $3.20, then when I become CEO it dropped to $2.60 but we finished at $6.50. We had doubled the valuation of the company. Morale went up and every metric went up. Employee engagement was up in the eighties, which was the highest we had ever had. In retrospect I think I would have gone a bit faster. The organisation was probably further ahead than I was, and I would have been bolder in some of the changes. I probably reflected too much about it and I probably would have spent a bit more money earlier-on to fix some of the problems we had. I think the principle of using the voice of the customer, or the market, to drive change, and really instilling it so that it's in every conversation, is incredibly powerful. It drives innovation, and re-invention. You're in this constant mode of creating a learning organisation.

Toll Group

Shane O'Neill: I don't think we were brutal enough with the Business Unit heads in the accountabilities and the changes that we needed to make. They watered it down in terms of some of the changes and the impact. That buy-in or that lack of support then flows downhill to the people below, and then we see as soon as there's a conflict between Operations and your customer change programme, traditionally Operations will win out. You need leaders who can work with Operations and say it's going to be really hard but it's the right thing to do, and we will change whatever we need to change. The first time they hit a roadblock, that leader says that Operations are going to suffer because we're going to have to do this as it's the right thing to do customer-wise. Then the whole organisation sits up and takes notice.

Then their next direct reports make a change, their next reports et cetera. The time span of that trickle-down effect is directly proportional to the culture. If the culture is very anti-customer and more operational, then you're going to be fighting a lot longer than if their culture is 'Customers First' or we're very pro change. If your historic culture is "leave me alone, I'll just do what I think is important, and I'll get you the results you've asked for", then it's going to make change a lot more difficult. In hindsight what I should have done is to have stripped out every single one of my senior management team within six months. Then I should have changed the incentive structures straight away in terms of how people got rewarded, which was then done by business units. I would have moved it to a lot more around areas that drive teamwork and trust. We should have taken money off the table in terms of what we were reporting results wise and poured it into talent, poured it into training, poured it into continuous improvement. We would have had a completely different culture six or seven years down the track. We wanted our model to be the most efficient, the best transport operator in the southern hemisphere. We would make sure that it is the best in the world and improve and improve. If we want customers to come along for the ride, we need to do something fundamentally different.

References

Please note that the references listed are for published books referred to in the text, not for all sources mentioned in this book.

- 100 Ways to Motivate Others: How Great Leaders Can Produce Insane Results Without Driving People Crazy, 1980 by Steve Chandler, Scott Richardson
- ADKAR A Model for Change in Business, Government and Our Community, 2006 by Jeffrey M. Hiatt
- Chief Customer Officer 2.0: How to Build Your Customer-Driven Growth Engine, 2015 by Jeanne Bliss
- Execution: The Discipline of Getting Things Done, 2002 by Larry Bossidy, Ram Charan, Charles Burck
- Good to Great: Why Some Companies Make the Leap and Others Don't, 2001 by Jim Collins
- Key Account Management: The Definitive Guide, 2011 by Diana Woodburn, Malcolm McDonald
- Leading Change, 2012 by John P. Kotter
- Managing Successful Projects with PRINCE2, 2017 by The Stationery Office, Axelos Ltd
- Strategic Selling: The Unique Sales System Proven Successful by America's Best Companies, 1985 by Robert B. Miller, Stephen E. Heiman, Tad Tuleja
- Switch: How to Change Things When Change Is Hard, 2010 by Chip Heath, Dan Heath
- The Loyalty Effect: The Hidden Force Behind Growth, Profits, and Lasting Value, 1996 by Frederick F. Reichheld, Thomas Teal

- The Practice of Management, 2017 by Peter Drucker
- The Ultimate Question 2.0: How Net Promoter Companies Thrive in a Customer-Driven World, 2011 by Fred Reichheld, Rob Markey
- Top Management Strategy, 1980 by Benjamin B. Tregoe, John W. Zimmerman
- Understanding Organizations, 1993 by Charles Handy

Index